Carol Doak

60 Fabulous Paper-Pieced Stars

2ND EDITION

✳ Includes 10 New National Park Blocks ✳

C&T PUBLISHING
Another Maker Inspired!

Text copyright © 2023 by Carol Doak

Photography and artwork copyright © 2023 by C&T Publishing, Inc.

Publisher: Amy Barrett-Daffin

Creative Director: Gailen Runge

Senior Editor: Roxane Cerda

Editors: Liz Aneloski and Gailen Runge

Technical Editor: Kathryn Patterson

Cover/Book Designer: April Mostek

Production Coordinator: Zinnia Heinzmann

Illustrator: Kirstie Pettersen

Photography by C&T Publishing, Inc., unless otherwise noted

Published by C&T Publishing, Inc., P.O. Box 1456, Lafayette, CA 94549

Library of Congress Cataloging-in-Publication Data

Names: Doak, Carol, author.

Title: 60 fabulous paper-pieced stars : includes 10 new national parks blocks / Carol Doak.

Other titles: 50 fabulous paper-pieced stars | Sixty fabulous paper-pieced stars

Description: 2nd edition. | Lafayette, CA : C&T Publishing, 2023. | Revised edition of: 50 fabulous paper-pieced stars / Carol Doak. 2000. | Summary: This second edition of Carol Doak's Fabulous Paper Pieced Stars includes updated information all new fabrics, illustrations, and photography and 10 new blocks based on the national parks. Readers will receive tips for using precuts, full-size paper piecing patterns, and step-by-step instructions on paper piecing-- Provided by publisher.

Identifiers: LCCN 2023009990 | ISBN 9781644034026 (trade paperback) | ISBN 9781644034033 (ebook)

Subjects: LCSH: Patchwork--Patterns. | Patchwork quilts. | Stars in art.

Classification: LCC TT835 .D59 2023 | DDC 746.46/041--dc23/eng/20230327

LC record available at https://lccn.loc.gov/2023009990

Printed in China

10 9 8 7 6 5 4 3 2

CONTENTS

Preface and Introduction ✳ **4**

Gathering Tools and Supplies ✳ **5**

Using Paper Foundations and Block-Front Drawings ✳ **6**

Selecting Fabrics and Creative Options ✳ **8**
Working with Grain Line and Directional Fabric ✳ 8
Exploring Creative Fabric Options ✳ 9
Mixing and Matching Sections ✳ 9

Paper-Piecing Techniques ✳ **10**
Measuring Fabric-Piece Size ✳ 10
Cutting Fabric Pieces ✳ 11
Calculating Yardage ✳ 12
Step-by-Step Paper Piecing ✳ 13
Sewing Assembly-Line Fashion ✳ 16
Fixing Mistakes ✳ 16

Completing the Block ✳ **17**
Joining Sections A and B ✳ 17
Adding Fabric Across Sections A and B ✳ 18
Joining the Sections ✳ 18
Removing the Paper ✳ 19

The Blocks ✳ **20**

Gallery of Stars ✳ **21**

50 State Star Blocks ✳ **24**

Bonus: 10 National Park Star Blocks ✳ **124**

About the Author ✳ **144**

Preface and Introduction

This second edition of the best-selling *50 Fabulous Paper-Pieced Stars* is a wonderful opportunity to make this book available to quilters of today and for years to come. It also allowed me to remake the original blocks in contemporary fabrics and add value to this book by adding ten bonus blocks to this collection. I have to share with you that remaking these blocks was as exciting this time as it was twenty years ago. When I finished each new block, I would hold it up and compare it to the original. "Wow, wow, and wow" often came from my mouth! Having the opportunity to create new blocks also produced a similar response. I hope you are as wowed with this second edition as I was.

It was a simple beginning—divide the LeMoyne Star into eight sections so that beginning quilters could easily piece it. As I looked at the sections, however, it occurred to me that each of them could be broken down further into paper-pieced units. I never dreamed this concept would give birth to so many fabulous paper-pieced star designs.

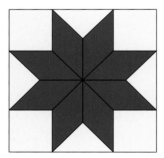
Traditional
LeMoyne Star block

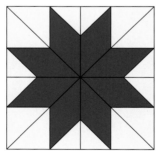
LeMoyne Star block
in eight sections

I decided to name each of the original 50 Star blocks for each of the 50 US states. The 10 bonus blocks are an opportunity to offer new exciting designs many years later. These new blocks are named after some of our national treasures, our national parks. Going back to remake the blocks in contemporary fabrics and add new designs has been so much fun.

Each of the 12″ blocks in this book is created from eight paper-pieced sections. The designs may look intricate, but paper piecing makes it possible to sew these designs with absolute precision. After you've made just one star block, I think you will see how great this technique really is.

1. Start with 2 triangle sections.

2. Join the triangles to make squares.

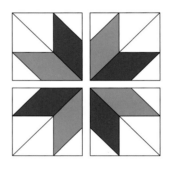

3. Join the squares to finish the block.

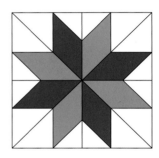

In Gathering Tools and Supplies (page 5), you will learn what items you need to make the blocks and reproduce the foundations for paper piecing. In Using Paper Foundations and Block-Front Drawings (page 6), you'll learn that you can use a copy machine or scanner to reproduce the foundations or enlarge or reduce the paper foundations to make star blocks in a variety of sizes.

In Selecting Fabrics and Creative Options (page 8), you will explore opportunities for choosing and using fabrics to create your star blocks. In the 50 State Star Blocks (page 24) and Bonus: 10 National Park Star Blocks (page 124), you will find a detailed cutting list for making one of each of the 12″ star blocks, plus color photos to inspire you. Use just one block design to make your project, or incorporate a variety of block designs. Either way, they offer the beginning of a whole new galaxy for years to come.

GATHERING TOOLS AND SUPPLIES

Having the right tool to do the job can mean the difference between fun and frustration. The following items will make paper piecing the star blocks fun.

6″ Add-A-Quarter™ Ruler: This tool is invaluable for pre-trimming the fabric pieces.

Utility knife (such as an X-Acto knife): Use this tool to undo seams easily.

Open-toe presser foot: This foot provides good visibility so you can see the line as you are stitching. If you don't have one, don't worry, you can still paper piece. It's just a "nice to have" item.

Carol Doak's Foundation Papers (by C&T Publishing): Use this lightweight paper when you copy the foundation piecing designs. It holds up during the sewing process and removes easily.

Postcard or card stock: Use a sturdy postcard or card stock to fold the paper back on the foundation before trimming the fabric pieces. The card that comes with the Carol Doak Foundation Paper is perfect for this purpose.

Rotary cutter and rotary mat: The large rotary cutter is the most effective with these star patterns because you will often be cutting through four layers of fabric and paper.

Rotary rulers: The 6″ × 12″ and the 6″ × 6″ rotary rulers are helpful for cutting the fabric and trimming the sections.

Scotch brand removable tape: This tape will be your new best friend if you need to repair your paper foundation.

Sewing thread: Use a standard 50-weight sewing thread. Match the thread color to the value of the fabrics. White, medium gray, and black can be used for most blocks. If both dark and light values are used equally, choose the darker thread.

Flat-headed pins: Use these to hold the fabric pieces in place. The flat head will not get in your way when trimming.

Size 90/14 sewing machine needles: The larger needle will help to perforate the paper so it is easy to remove later.

Small light: This will be helpful when you want to center a fabric element in the #1 position and see through the foundation.

Small stick-on notes: Label your stacks of cut fabric pieces with these. They will keep you organized and save you time.

Curved pointed snips: These are great for removing the top and bottom threads simultaneously. From the paper side, pull up the thread to bring up the bottom thread and snip.

Tweezers: These will come in handy to remove the tiny bits of paper.

Using Paper Foundations and Block-Front Drawings

Each star block requires four copies of each of the section A and B triangles. One way to make paper foundations is to photocopy the designs on a copy machine. Be sure to make all the copies for your project with the same copy machine from the original designs. For a nominal fee, most copy shops will remove the binding of this book and three-hole-punch the pages or spiral bind it to make using it on a copy machine even easier. If you have a scanner, you can also scan the foundation page into your device and print your foundations. Always test the accuracy of the copy or scan before using it.

You can also reduce and enlarge the designs on a copy machine or print a scanned image larger or smaller to create the star blocks in a variety of sizes. The photograph at left shows the Delaware Star in the original 12″ size, as well as 4″, 6″, 8″, and 15″ to illustrate the creative opportunities enlarging and reducing the designs offer.

Use the following chart to determine reduction and enlargement percentages:

Finished Size Star Block	Finished Size Triangle Section	Enlargement or Reduction % of original
15″	7½″	125%
14″	7″	117%
13″	6½″	108%
12″	6″	100%*
11″	5½″	92%
10″	5″	83%
9″	4½″	75%
8″	4″	67%
7″	3½″	58%
6″	3″	50%
4″	2″	33%

Original Size

The paper you use for foundation piecing should hold up while sewing and be easy to remove. If in doubt, test your paper by sewing through it with a size 90/14 needle and a stitch length of 18 to 20 stitches per inch. If it tears as you sew, it is too weak. If it doesn't tear easily when pulled after sewing, it is too strong. The paper does not need to be translucent. The light from your sewing machine is sufficient to see through the blank size of the paper to the lines on the other side. *Carol Doak's Foundation Paper* (by C&T Publishing) works beautifully for these star blocks.

After you make 4 copies of sections A and B, cut the triangles ½″ from the outside solid line. To do this quickly and easily, pin the center of the sections together using a flat-headed pin. Use your rotary ruler and cutter to trim. You do not dull your blade doing this if you use *Carol Doak's Foundation Paper.* Remove the pin.

The small block-front drawings at the bottom of the pattern pages show how the star blocks will appear when they are completed. Use these blocks to experiment with color and design choices. One set of decisions can result in a very different star block from another set of decisions. The block-front drawings are the reverse image of the foundations.

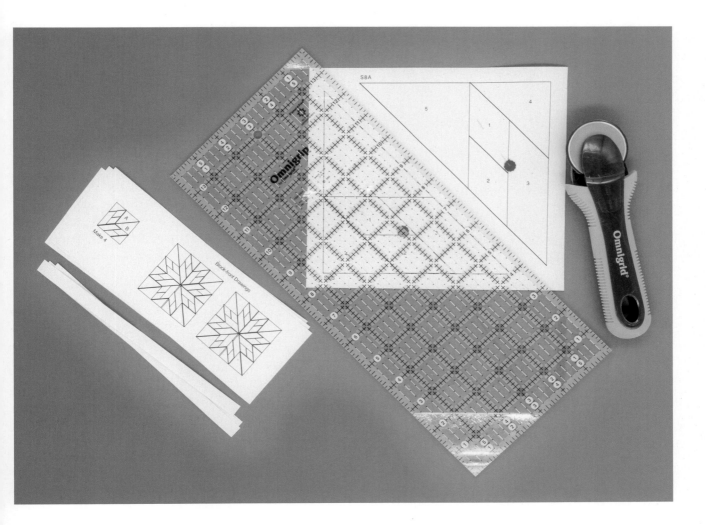

Using Paper Foundations and Block-Front Drawings

Selecting Fabrics and Creative Options

Your fabric choices will bring your paper-pieced blocks to life, but it is good to know what options you have.

Working with Grain Line and Directional Fabric

Because you are paper piecing, you do not need to concern yourself with fabric grain for mechanical reasons. The paper supports the fabric no matter how it is placed on the foundation. Visually, however, the grain line and the print on the fabric do have an impact on the finished block. For this reason, the background triangles are cut as half-square triangles so that the grain line and the print will be consistent along the edges of the block. The larger the fabric pieces, the more important it is to keep this consistency.

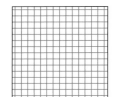

Start with a square of background fabric.

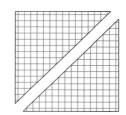

Cut it in half to make half-square triangles.

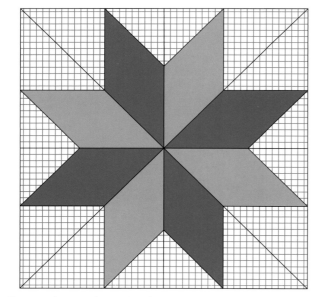

Position the triangles so that the grain line and printed pattern are consistent throughout the block.

Select non-directional fabrics when the fabric will be used along various directional seam lines. The white fabric below illustrates this point.

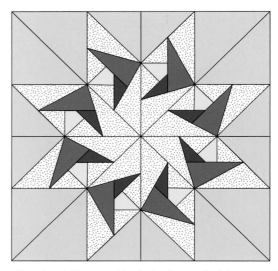

Non-directional fabric used in the background of the star points

You may select directional fabric when placed on the same seam line direction. The stripe fabric below illustrates this point.

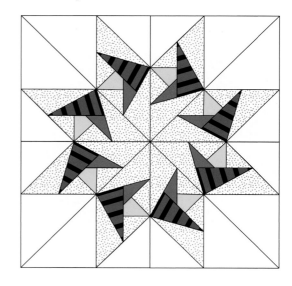

Exploring Creative Fabric Options

Your choice of fabrics can set a theme, create a graphic impact or add extra detail to your star block. I often start by selecting the fabric for the background of the star. Frequently I look for a "main player" fabric that I love and then select the remainder of the fabrics based on the colors in that fabric.

Because many of the cut pieces in the star blocks are under 2″ wide, jelly rolls are a great way to have a variety of fabric pieces to use in the star blocks. Fat quarters work well for the background triangles.

Or you may just choose a color grouping like greens and blues, a neutral, and lots of colors. The bottom line is to choose fabrics that make your heart sing. You can experiment by coloring in the block-front drawings with your color choices to achieve the look you desire.

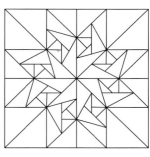

S30 New Jersey

S1 Alabama

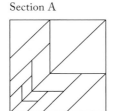

Section A

Section B

Mixing and Matching Sections

The star blocks in this book are just the beginning of your creative opportunities. Since the A sections are interchangeable and the B Sections are interchangeable, you have the opportunity to combine an A section from one block with a B section from a different block to create a new star design. Use the block-front drawings to experiment with options. The following example shows the block-front drawings from Alabama and Delaware combined.

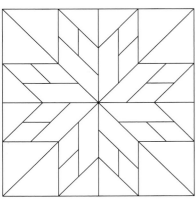

S8 Delaware

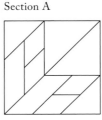

Section A

Section B

New star block

S1-A Alabama

S8-B Delaware

Paper-Piecing Techniques

Measuring Fabric-Piece Size

The good news is that there is a cutting list for making one of each 12″ star block. The measurements are generous to allow room for easy placement and any shifting that might occur while you sew.

However, if you decide to enlarge or reduce the designs, you will want to know how to measure the fabric pieces. To measure the first piece, place a rotary ruler over the area marked #1 in the same way you will place the #1 fabric. You can see how big the fabric piece needs to be, including a generous seam allowance. I allow at least ¾″ total for seam allowances. Write the measurement on your foundation.

To measure the subsequent fabric pieces, place the ¼″ line on the rotary ruler on the seam you will sew and let the ruler fall over the area of the next piece. Add ½″ on the opposing side. Look through the ruler to see how big the piece needs to be, including a generous seam allowance on all sides. Write the measurement on your foundation.

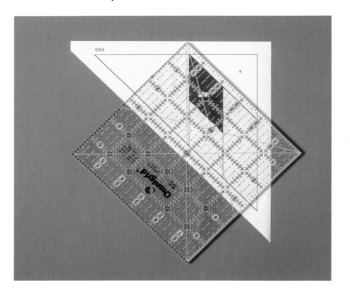

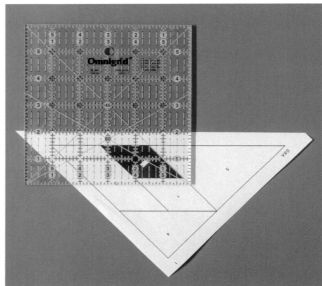

For the half-square triangles, measure the short side of the triangle and add 1¼″ to that measurement. Cut a square the size of the short side of the triangle plus 1¼″ and cut it once diagonally.

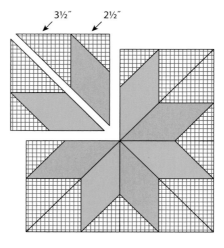

When the short side measures 3½″, add 1¼″ for seam allowances to cut a square 4¾″ × 4¾″. Cut in half diagonally to make two half-square triangles.

When the short side measures 2½″, add 1¼″ for seam allowances to cut a square 3¾″ × 3¾″. Cut in half diagonally to make two half-square triangles.

Cutting Fabric Pieces

Once your fabric is selected, it is time to rotary cut your fabric pieces. Remember, each star block has a cutting list. If you prefer different colors from the ones listed, simply substitute your fabric choices for the ones in the chart. And if you want to cut your pieces larger to give yourself more wiggle room with placement, that is fine, too.

To cut several pieces at one time, fold the fabric twice and cut a strip across the width. If you need only a few pieces, cut a shorter strip.

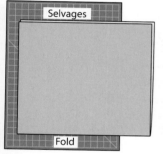

Fabric folded once

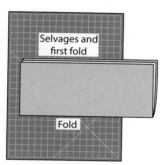

Fabric folded twice to cut strips

As the pieces are cut, label them with stick-on notes to indicate the location number and section. Since the fabric is folded, the pieces will be right side up and wrong side up. Take the time to arrange them so they are all right side up. This saves time when sewing.

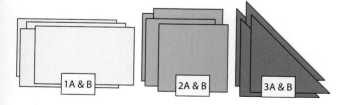

Many of the star blocks require half-square triangles for the background triangles. These are easily cut from 4¾″ and 3¾″ squares. Fold the fabric twice and cut a 4¾″-wide strip across the width. Turn the strip and remove the fold and selvage edges. Cut four squares 4¾″ × 4¾″. Remember, since you're cutting four layers of fabric at a time, you will be cutting four squares at once. Cut the squares once diagonally to make eight triangles. Cut four squares, 3¾″ × 3¾″, from the remainder of the strip, and cut once diagonally to make eight triangles.

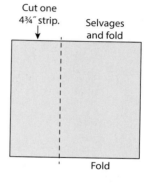

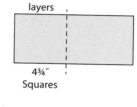

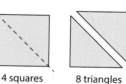

If you decide to use a one-way directional fabric for the background triangles, cut the squares from a strip as described on page 11. With like sides together (either right sides or wrong sides), cut the squares once diagonally. Paper piece the eight sections but do not add the background triangles. Lay out the A and B sections to form the star. Then position the triangles so the print is oriented correctly. Stitch the triangles in place.

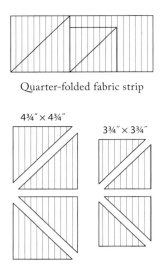

Quarter-folded fabric strip

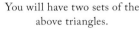

You will have two sets of the above triangles.

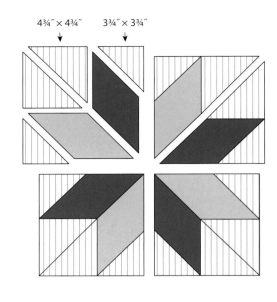

After the fabric pieces are cut and labeled, place them on a tray in numerical order. This allows you to move them from the cutting area to the sewing machine area easily. I find that the trays you often get fruit and meats on at the supermarket are perfect for this purpose. Be sure to wash them well.

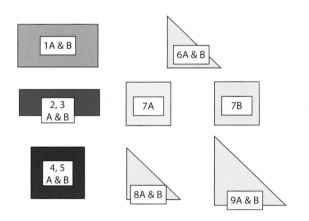

Calculating Yardage

When I wrote the first book, I often received emails asking how to calculate yardage for a full quilt of one block. Here is how you would calculate yardage when making multiples of the same block. I will use 12 blocks and the light blue print in the Alabama block for my example. One block requires 8 pieces, each 1½″ × 2½″.

1. Determine the number of pieces for 1 block and then multiply by 12 blocks; 8 pieces × 12 blocks equals 96 pieces needed.

2. Each piece is 1½″ × 2½″. Determine how many pieces 2½″ long you can cut from a 40″ strip. 40″ divided by 2½″ equals 16 pieces.

3. Divide the 96 pieces needed by 16 pieces to determine the number of 1½″ strips to cut. The answer is 6 strips. If the answer was less than a whole number, round up.

4. Multiply 6 strips times 1½″ to determine the yardage needed. The answer is 9″ which is exactly ¼ yard. I would typically round up to give myself a bit extra, so I would purchase ⅓ yard or 12″. If you were cutting multiple pieces from the same fabric, add the amounts together and then determine yardage.

Step-by-Step Paper Piecing

With your foundations copied and trimmed, your fabric selected, cut, and labeled, you are now ready to begin paper piecing the sections for your star block. The numbered and lined side of the foundation is the reverse (or mirror image) of the finished block. This often confuses beginners to paper piecing because they look at the lined side and try to think in reverse. The key is to look through the blank side of the foundation to the lines on the other side. This way, what you see is what you get and you do not need to think in reverse.

In the following photographs, translucent tracing paper is used as the foundation for the Delaware Star block, Section A, so you can see the lines through the blank side of the paper.

1. Use a size 90/14 sewing machine needle, an open-toe presser foot for good visibility, and a stitch length of 18 to 20 stitches to the inch. The larger needle and smaller stitch length will aid you in removing the paper easily.

2. Using the light on your sewing machine (or an additional light source), look through the **blank side** of the paper to place fabric piece #1 **right side up** over the area marked #1. Looking through the lined side, make sure it covers area #1 and extends at least ¼″ beyond all seam lines. Pin in place. I always pin parallel to the seam line I will sew.

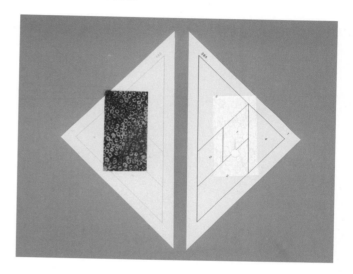

3. Place the postcard on the line between #1 and #2 over the #1 area, and fold the paper back to expose the excess fabric beyond the seam line.

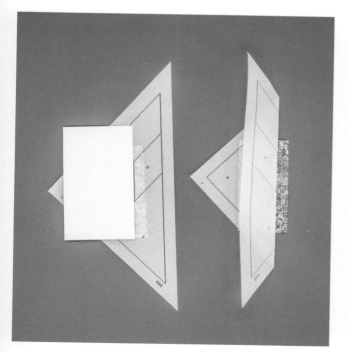

4. Place an Add-a-Quarter ruler on the fold and trim the excess fabric ¼″ from the fold. The lip on this ruler prevents it from slipping as you trim. You can also align the ¼″ on a rotary ruler with the fold to trim.

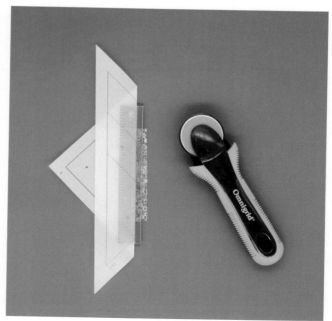

5. Looking through the blank side of the paper to the design on the other side, place fabric #2 **right** side up over area #2. This step allows you to ballpark the placement of the #2 fabric.

After piece #2 is properly positioned, flip it right sides together with the just-trimmed edge of piece #1. Looking through the blank side of the paper again, check that the end of #2 extends beyond the end of the seam line of #2 on the foundation. Pin in place.

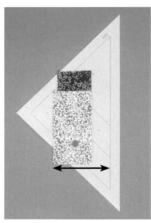

6. Place the foundation under the presser foot and sew on the seam line between #1 and #2, beginning about ½″ before the seam and extending the stitching the same distance beyond the end of the seam line.

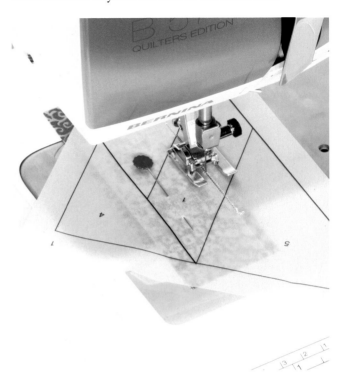

7. Remove the pin and open piece #2. Press with a dry iron on a cotton setting. If you are using heat-sensitive fabrics, use a pressing cloth or lower the temperature of the iron. Cover your ironing surface with a piece of scrap fabric to protect it from any ink that may transfer from photocopies. If you are getting much transfer, reduce the temperature. Caution: Never press the printed side of the foundation as the iron will smear the ink.

8. Place the postcard on the next line you will sew. This is where line #3 adjoins the previous pieces. Fold the paper back exposing the excess fabric. If necessary, pull the extending stitches away from the paper foundation to fold the paper. Place the Add-a-Quarter ruler on the fold and trim ¼″ from the fold.

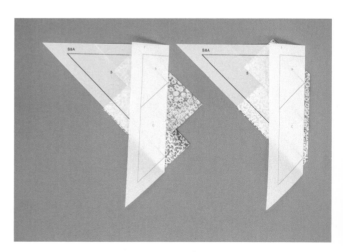

9. Place fabric #3 **right** side up over area #3 to check for proper placement. Place the fabric right sides together with the just-trimmed edges of pieces #1 and #2. See how the fabric extends to cover the center point of the section plus seam allowance? Sew and press open.

10. Continue with piece #4 by placing the postcard on the line between #1/#3 and #4. Fold the paper back and trim the excess fabrics ¼" from the fold. Place triangle #4 **right** side up over area #4 to check for placement, and then flip it right sides together along the just-trimmed edge. Align the corner of the fabric triangle with the corner of the triangle printed on the foundation. Sew and press open.

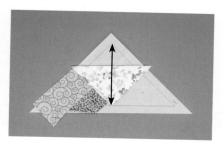

11. Place the postcard on the line between #1/#2 and #5. Fold the paper back and trim the excess fabric ¼" from the fold. Place triangle #5 **right** side up over area #5 to check for placement and then flip it right sides together along the just-trimmed edge. Center the triangle so the edge extends at least ¼" beyond the outside line. Sew and press open.

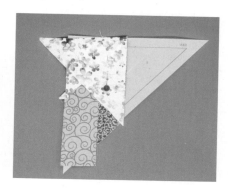

12. Trim the foundation ¼" from the outside SOLID line as follows.

A. Trim the long side of the triangle first.

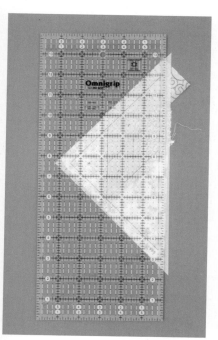

B. Next trim the right-hand side of the triangle.

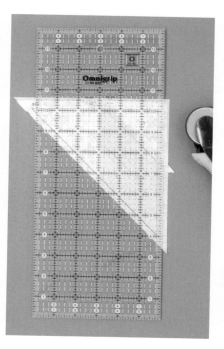

C. Lastly, trim the final side of the triangle.

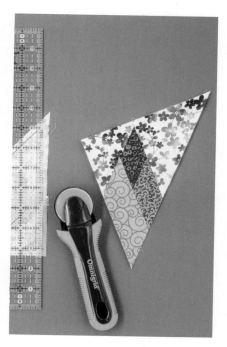

Sewing Assembly-Line Fashion

It is much more efficient to assembly-line sew the A sections first, and then sew the B sections. If this is your first paper piecing experience, make one of each section first before you begin assembly-line sewing.

To sew the A sections in assembly-line fashion, pin all the #1 pieces in place and trim them. Stack the foundations the same way. Position piece #2 and sew the first seam line. Pull the foundation away from the needle area, and then position and sew piece #2 on the next foundation. Again, place all the #2 pieces the same way. Continue until all the #2 pieces have been sewn. Following a routine, by positioning all the foundations and the pieces to sew in the same way, helps to speed things up because you are not rethinking each step.

Bring all the foundations to the ironing board and clip the top threads on the paper side, pulling up the bobbin thread to clip at the same time using the curved pointed snips. Press all the #2 pieces open. Continue by trimming the #2 pieces to add the next pieces.

Fixing Mistakes

It's easy to fix a mistake should you need to remove a piece. Place a piece of Scotch Brand removable tape on the seam line where you will remove the piece. The tape will keep the paper intact. From the fabric side, lift the piece to be removed until the stitches at the end of the seam are visible. Lightly touch the stitches with the utility knife to cut them as you keep upward pressure on the fabric being removed. Once the piece is removed, you can resew the seam and the tape is your new foundation. Caution: Do not touch the tape with your iron.

COMPLETING THE BLOCK

Joining Sections A and B

When the A and B sections are completed and trimmed, it is time to join them to make quarter blocks. With section B facing you, place the A and B sections together, right sides facing. Place the long side down on a hard surface to align them. Hold the papers firmly and pin the right-angle corner.

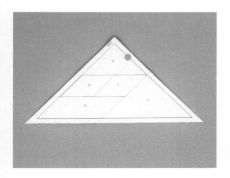

Walk your fingers along the long sides to align them and pin at the beginning, at each matching point or every 3˝, and at the endpoint. Place pins away from the seam lines. Place one more pin in the middle of the block.

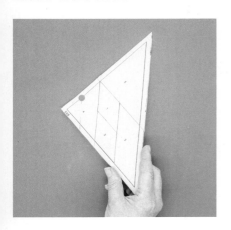

Trust me, you'll definitely want to follow this basting step before you join the sections with a small stitch. Basting allows you to check that the seams match before you sew them and it prevents the sections from shifting.

To baste, increase the stitch length to about eight stitches per inch. With section B facing up, baste about one inch on the line at the beginning of the line, move to any matching points or every 3 inches if there are no matching points along the seam, and at the end.

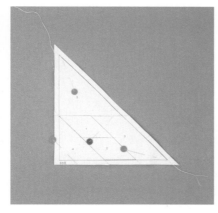

Remove the basted triangles from the sewing machine and check that you have basted on the seam line of Section A. Open up the sections and check for a good match. If they are good, sew with the small stitch. If one or more is not good, clip the basting thread for that seam, adjust and baste again until the match is

good, and then sew with the small stitch.

Clip the seam allowances at an angle to reduce bulk where the centers and corners will come together.

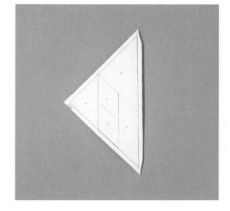

With section B on top, open and press the seam allowances toward section B from the fabric side.

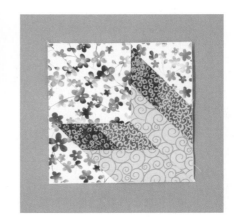

Adding Fabric Across Sections A and B

Some of the star blocks have additional pieces of fabric that need to be sewn across sections A and B after the sections are joined. This is indicated on the block foundation and in the cutting list with an asterisk (*) following the number. When a block calls for this option, follow these steps:

1. Trim the last piece on each section ¼″ from the next seam line. In the following example, the #6 pieces were trimmed ¼″ from the line. This is an important step because you cannot trim after the sections are joined.

2. Trim the A and B sections ¼″ from the outside **solid** line of the triangle.

3. Pin the A and B sections right sides together, making sure that the sewing lines meet for the pieces to be sewn across both sections. Baste, check, and sew the diagonal seam.

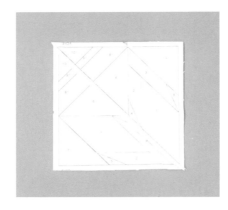

4. Continue foundation piecing across the joined sections. The following photograph shows pieces

#8, #9 and #10 in position ready to be flipped right sides together and sewn in sequence across the joined A and B sections.

5. When the fabric pieces have been added, trim the added fabric pieces ¼″ from the outside solid line.

Joining the Sections

Join the four quarters for one star block in the same way.

Place two quarters right sides together in the correct position. Pin; baste at the beginning, at any matching points or every 3″ if there are no matching points, and at the end; check for a good match.

When you are happy with the match, sew with a small stitch. Join the remaining two quarters. Press the seam allowance for both sets in the same direction. You now have two halves of a star.

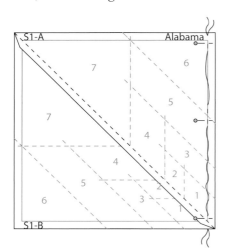

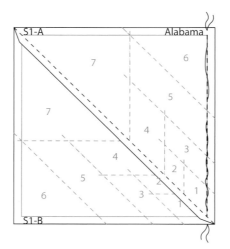

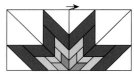

Make two halves. Press seam allowances from the fabric side in the same direction to the right.

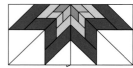

Middle seam allowances will go in opposite directions.

With right sides facing, pin the two halves together. Pin each end. Pin the matching points from the ends to the middle. Pin the middle last with seam allowances going in opposite directions. Baste at the beginning, at any matching points or every 3 inches if there are no matching points, and at the end. Check you have a good match, and sew with a smaller stitch. I found that if I decreased the stitch length to twenty-five stitches per inch just at the center seam, it gave an even tighter match. From the back of the paper side, finger press the final seam in opposite directions following the spiral of the seam allowances. Turn the block to the fabric side and press.

Removing the Paper

Do not remove the paper until the block is joined to other blocks or other straight-grain fabric pieces. The outside seam lines act as a sewing guide and the paper stabilizes the blocks. To remove the paper, begin at the center portion of the block and gently tug diagonally to pull the paper away from the stitching lines. Use tweezers to remove any caught paper. You can ignore really tiny bits.

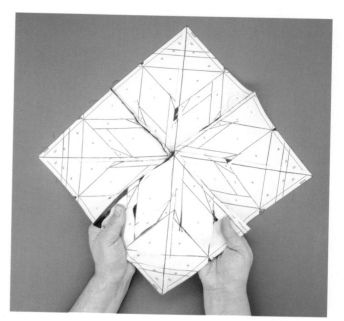

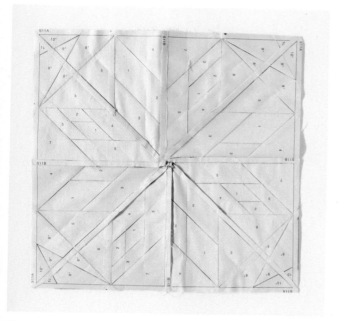

Finger press the middle seam in opposite directions to follow the spiral of seam allowances on the back of the block.

THE BLOCKS

The Gallery of Stars (page 21) presents all sixty star blocks together. Use these pages to pick out the star you want to make. The first fifty blocks represent US states. The last ten blocks represent US National Parks.

Following the Gallery of Stars, you'll see photographs and a cutting list for each of the star blocks. Digital reproductions were made of the star block photography to show how four blocks will look when joined. Several blocks have background patchwork elements that make secondary designs when joined, and these digital reproductions illustrate that.

To indicate the time investment required, the number of pieces in each block is shown. A block of forty pieces can be made in half the time of a block that contains eighty pieces. The blocks with more pieces are not more difficult, they just are more time-consuming but well worth it in the end.

The cutting list provided for each star block is for making one block. If you use different colors but the same fabric placements, follow the list substituting your color choice.

The ◻ symbol in the cutting list indicates to cut the squares once diagonally to create two half-square triangles (see pages 11–12). An asterisk (*) following a number indicates fabric pieces that are sewn after the A and B sections have been joined (see page 18). The foundation pages include a full-size paper piecing foundation for each block. They are the reverse image of the finished block. Each section is labeled A or B and S (for star) and the number of the block. S1-A is the A foundation for the first block, Alabama. Make four copies each of A and B to make one block (see pages 6–7).

On the bottom are the block-front drawings to show how the completed A and B quarter sections will be and then two copies of the finished blocks. You can use these to experiment with color placements (page 9) or mix and match sections (page 9).

Number of Pieces	Star Blocks
40	8, 16
48	6, 17
52	27
56	1, 19, 20, 21, 26, 46, 49, 60
60	7, 11, 28
64	12, 14, 23, 32, 37, 38, 39, 42, 44, 45, 47, 51
68	25, 43
72	3, 30, 31, 33, 35, 50, 52, 55, 57, 59
80	10, 18, 24
88	34, 53, 56
96	5, 29
100	41, 54
104	2, 4, 13
108	48
112	9, 15
120	40
128	22, 36, 58

S1 Alabama

S2 Alaska

S3 Arizona

S4 Arkansas

S5 California

S6 Colorado

S7 Connecticut

S8 Delaware

S9 Florida

S10 Georgia

S11 Hawaii

S12 Idaho

S13 Illinois

S14 Indiana

S15 Iowa

S16 Kansas

S17 Kentucky

S18 Louisiana

S19 Maine

S20 Maryland

GALLERY OF STARS

S21 Massachusetts

S22 Michigan

S23 Minnesota

S24 Mississippi

S25 Missouri

S26 Montana

S27 Nebraska

S28 Nevada

S29 New Hampshire

S30 New Jersey

S31 New Mexico

S32 New York

S33 North Carolina

S34 North Dakota

S35 Ohio

S36 Oklahoma

S37 Oregon

S38 Pennsylvania

S39 Rhode Island

S40 South Carolina

S41 South Dakota

S42 Tennessee

S43 Texas

S44 Utah

S45 Vermont

S46 Virginia

S47 Washington

S48 West Virginia

S49 Wisconsin

S50 Wyoming

S51 Acadia

S52 Denali

S53 Everglades

S54 Glacier

S55 Grand Canyon

S56 Mt. Rainier

S57 Redwood

S58 Rocky Mountain

S59 Yellowstone

S60 Zion

~ STAR BLOCK 1 ~
Alabama Star

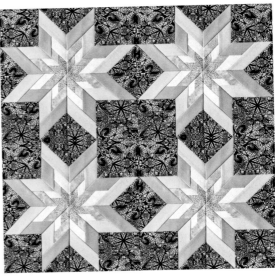

56 PIECES

The following fabric cutting list is for one star block.

Fabric	Number of Pieces	Piece Dimensions	Piece Number	Block Section
Light blue print	8	1½″ × 2½″	1	A, B
Light pink	4	1½″ × 2½″	2	A
	4	1½″ × 3½″	3	B
Medium pink	4	1½″ × 2½″	2	B
	4	1½″ × 3½″	3	A
Medium-light blue	4	1¾″ × 4″	4	A
	4	1¾″ × 6″	5	B
Medium blue	4	1¾″ × 4″	4	B
	4	1¾″ × 6″	5	A
Black print	4	3¾″ × 3¾″ ◫	6	A, B
	4	4¾″ × 4¾″ ◫	7	A, B

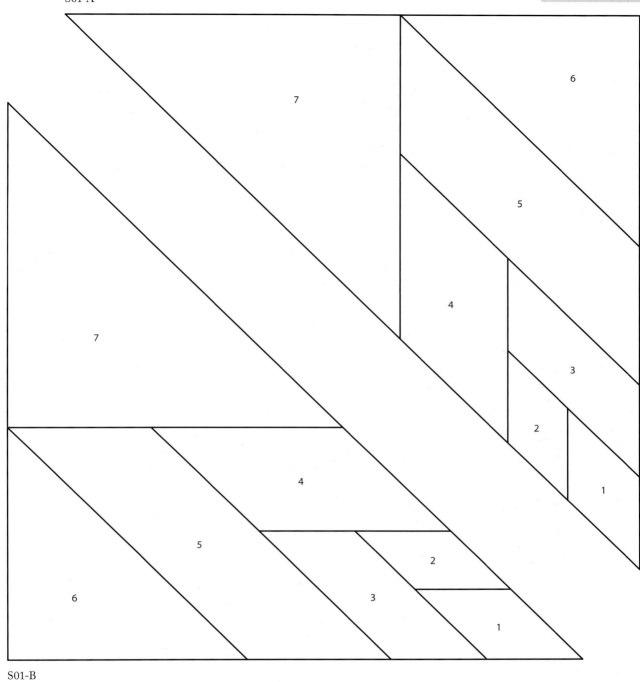

S01-A

7

6

5

4

7

3

2

1

S01-B

7

4

5

2

6

3

1

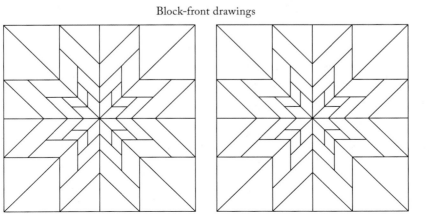

Block-front drawings

Make 4.

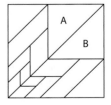

A

B

Alabama Star

～ STAR BLOCK 2 ～
Alaska Star

104 PIECES

The following fabric cutting list is for one star block.

Fabric	Number of Pieces	Piece Dimensions	Piece Number	Block Section
White	8	3″ × 3″ ◻	10, 11	A, B
	8	2¼″ × 2¼″ ◻	2, 3	A, B
	16	1½″ × 2½″	6, 7	A, B
Purple print	8	2″ × 3½″	1	A, B
Teal	16	1¼″ × 3½″	4, 5	A, B
Medium blue	16	1¼″ × 3½″	8, 9	A, B
Dark blue print	4	4¾″ × 4¾″ ◻	13	A, B
	4	3¾″ × 3¾″ ◻	12	A, B

S02-A

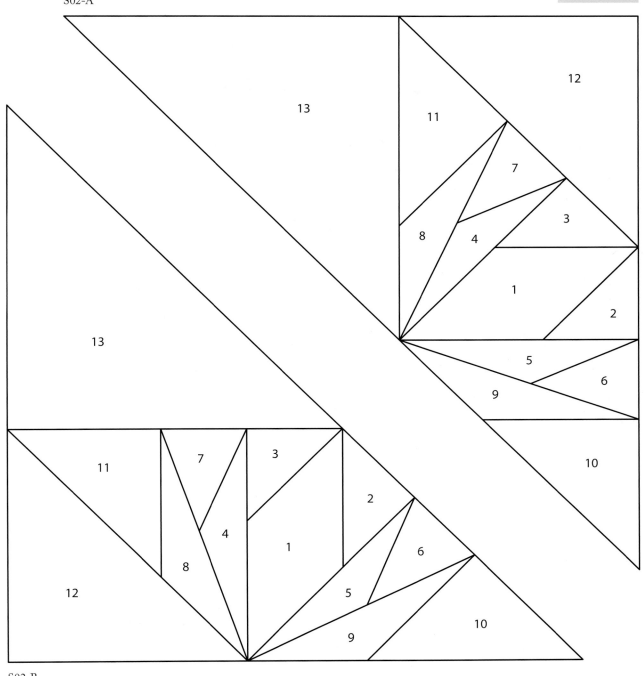

13

12

11

7

3

8

4

1

2

5

6

9

13

11

7

3

4

8

1

2

12

6

5

10

9

10

S02-B

Block-front drawings

Make 4.

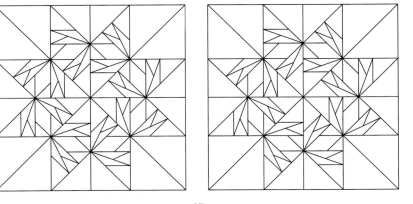

A

B

Alaska Star

✳ STAR BLOCK 3
Arizona Star

72 PIECES

The following fabric cutting list is for one star block.

Fabric	Number of Pieces	Piece Dimensions	Piece Number	Block Section
Gold	8	1″ × 1½″	1	A, B
Light teal	8	1¼″ × 2″	2	A, B
	8	1¼″ × 3″	3	A, B
Medium rust	8	2¼″ × 3″	4	A, B
Dark rust	8	2¼″ × 4″	5	A, B
Light green	8	1½″ × 3″	6	A, B
Dark green	8	2¾″ × 4″	7	A, B
Coral print	4	3¾″ × 3¾″ ◻	8	A, B
	4	4¾″ × 4¾″ ◻	9	A, B

S03-A

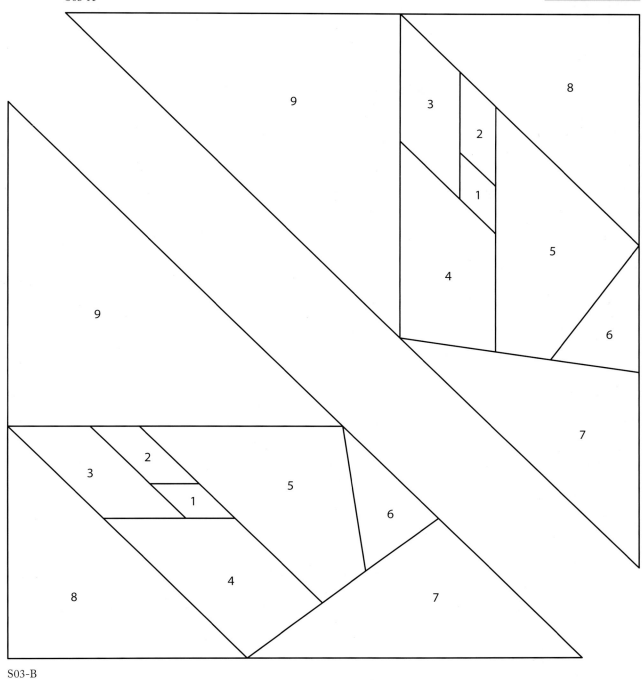

9

8

3

2

1

4

5

6

7

9

S03-B

3

2

1

5

6

4

8

7

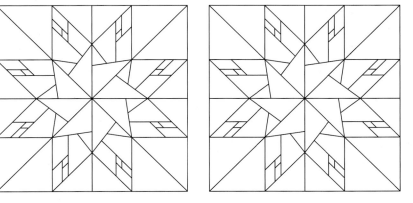

Block-front drawings

Make 4.

A

B

29

Arizona Star

Arkansas Star

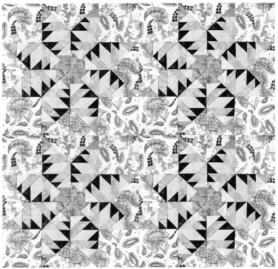

104 PIECES

The following fabric cutting list is for one star block.

Fabric	Number of Pieces	Piece Dimensions	Piece Number	Block Section
Yellow	8	1¾″ × 3½″	1	A, B
Pink	16	1½″ × 3½″	4, 5	A, B
Light green	8	2½″ × 2½″ ◻	8, 9	A, B
Medium green	8	2½″ × 2½″ ◻	10, 11	A, B
Dark purple	8	2½″ × 2½″ ◻	2, 3	A, B
	8	2″ × 2″ ◻	6, 7	A, B
White print	4	3¾″ × 3¾″ ◻	12	A, B
	4	4¾″ × 4¾″ ◻	13	A, B

S04-A

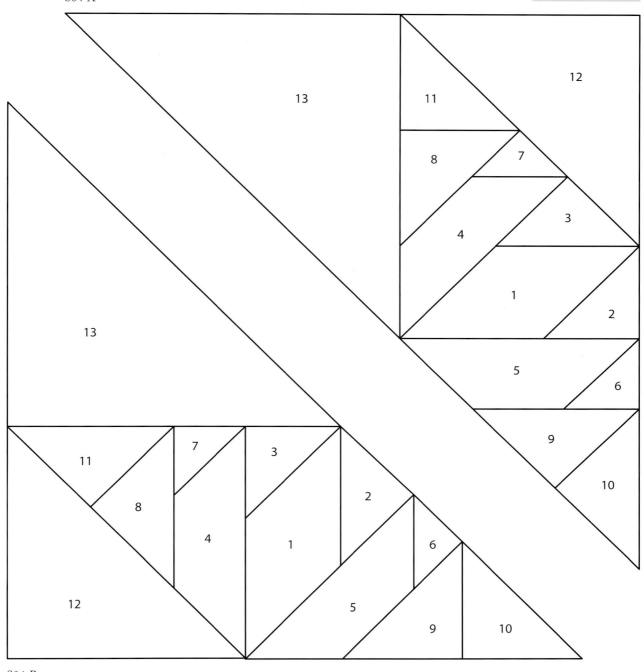

S04-B

Block-front drawings

Make 4.

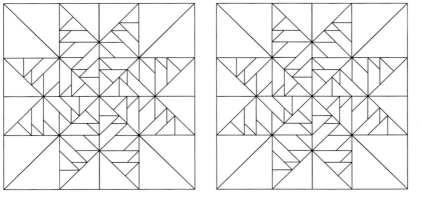

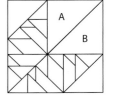

31

Arkansas Star

∽ STAR BLOCK 5 ∾
California Star

96 PIECES

The following fabric cutting list is for one star block.

Fabric	Number of Pieces	Piece Dimensions	Piece Number	Block Section
Stripe	8	2″ × 4″	1	A, B
Red	16	1¼″ × 3½″	4, 5	A, B
Black and red print	16	1½″ × 5″	8, 9	A, B
White	32	1″ × 4″	2, 3, 6, 7	A, B
Black and white print	8	2″ × 2″	10	A, B
	4	3¾″ × 3¾″ ◻	11	A, B
	4	4¾″ × 4¾″ ◻	12	A, B

S05-A

10

11

12

9

8

3

2

6

7

5

1

4

10

9

3

7

2

4

8

1

11

6

5

10

S05-B

Block-front drawings

Make 4.

A

B

California Star

⁓ STAR BLOCK 6 ⁓
Colorado Star

48 PIECES

The following fabric cutting list is for one star block.

Fabric	Number of Pieces	Piece Dimensions	Piece Number	Block Section
Green	4	2″ × 4″	1	A
	4	3½″ × 4″	4	A
Dark blue and green	4	2″ × 4″	1	B
	4	3½″ × 4″	4	B
White	16	2″ × 3″	2, 3	A, B
Yellow	4	3¾″ × 3¾″ ◻	5	A, B
	4	4¾″ × 4¾″ ◻	6	A, B

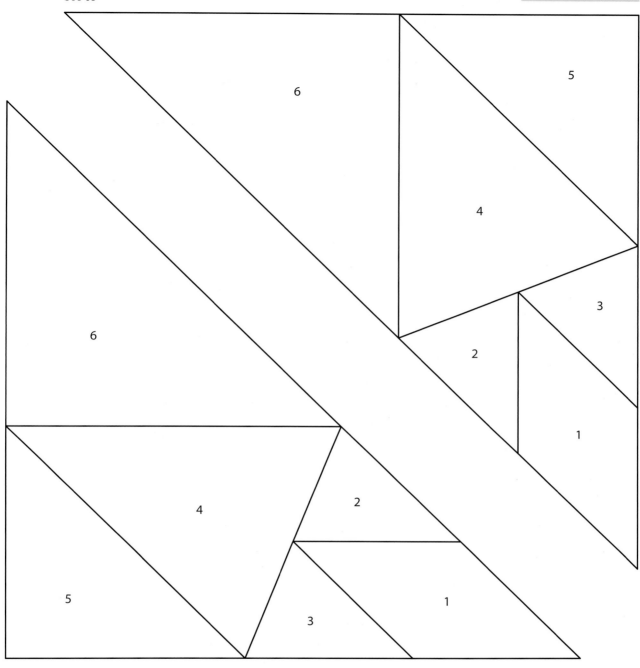

S06-A

6

5

4

6

3

2

1

S06-B

4

2

5

1

3

Block-front drawings

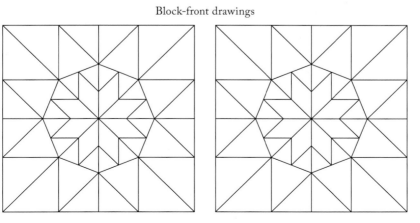

Make 4.

A

B

Colorado Star

~ STAR BLOCK 7 ~
# Connecticut Star

60 PIECES

The following fabric cutting list is for one star block.

Fabric	Number of Pieces	Piece Dimensions	Piece Number	Block Section
	4	2″ × 4″	1	B
	8	1″ × 4″	2, 3	A
Dark green	4	1½″ × 4½″	4	B
	4	1½″ × 6″	5	B
	4	2″ × 4″	1	A
	8	1″ × 4″	2, 3	B
Blue	4	1½″ × 4½″	4	A
	4	1½″ × 6″	5	A
Blue squares print	2	4¾″ × 4¾″ ◺	8*	A, B
Light blue print	8	3¾″ × 3¾″ ◺	6, 7	A, B

*Add these pieces after sections A and B are joined. See page 18.

36

60 Fabulous Paper-Pieced Stars, 2nd Edition

S07-A

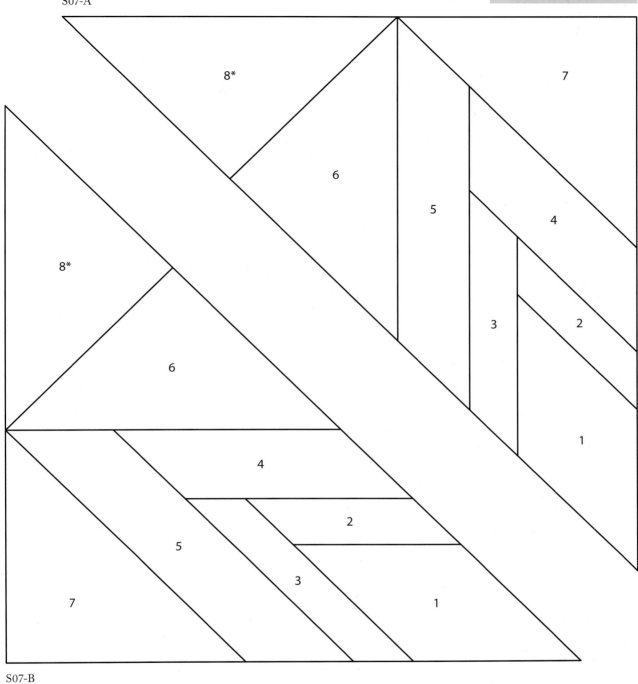

8*

7

6

5

4

8*

3

2

6

1

4

2

5

3

7

1

S07-B

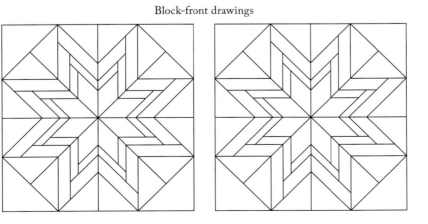

Block-front drawings

Make 4.

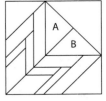

A

B

Connecticut Star

～ STAR BLOCK 8 ～
Delaware Star

40 PIECES

The following fabric cutting list is for one star block.

Fabric	Number of Pieces	Piece Dimensions	Piece Number	Block Section
Dark blue	8	2″ × 4″	1	A, B
Pink	8	2″ × 4″	2	A, B
Green	8	2″ × 6″	3	A, B
Floral print	4	3¾″ × 3¾″ ◻	4	A, B
	4	4¾″ × 4¾″ ◻	5	A, B

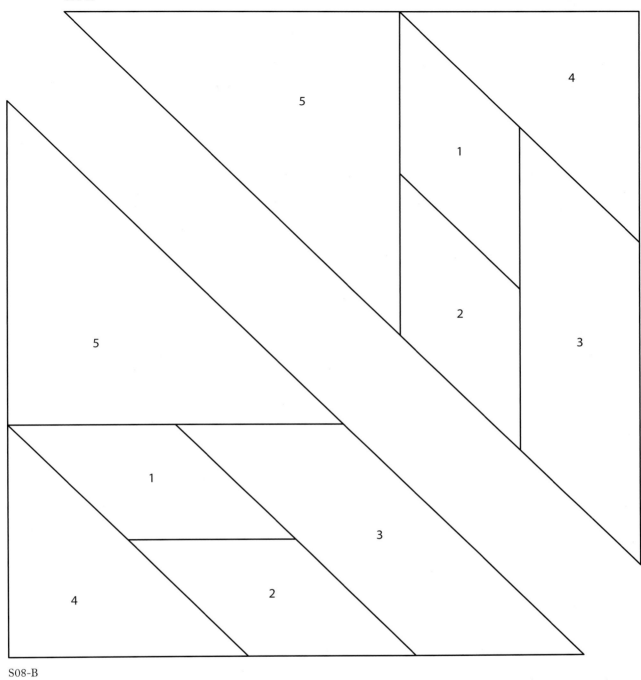

S08-A

S08-B

Block-front drawings

Make 4.

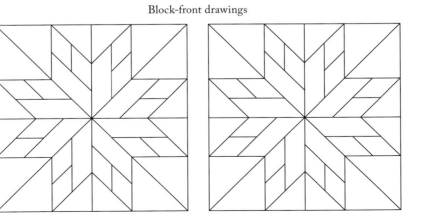

Delaware Star

~ STAR BLOCK 9 ~
Florida Star

112 PIECES

The following fabric cutting list is for one star block.

Fabric	Number of Pieces	Piece Dimensions	Piece Number	Block Section
Red #1	8	1¼″ × 3″	1	A, B
Red #2	8	1¼″ × 3″	3	A, B
Red #3	8	1¼″ × 3″	5	A, B
Red #4	8	1¼″ × 3″	7	A, B
Red #5	8	1¼″ × 3″	9	A, B
	32	1½″ × 2¼″	2, 4, 6, 8	A, B
Black	8	2″ × 2¼″	10	A, B
	8	2½″ × 4½″	12	A, B
Green	8	1¼″ × 2½″	11	A, B
White and grey print	4	3¾″ × 3¾″ ◻	13	A, B
	4	4¾″ × 4¾″ ◻	14	A, B

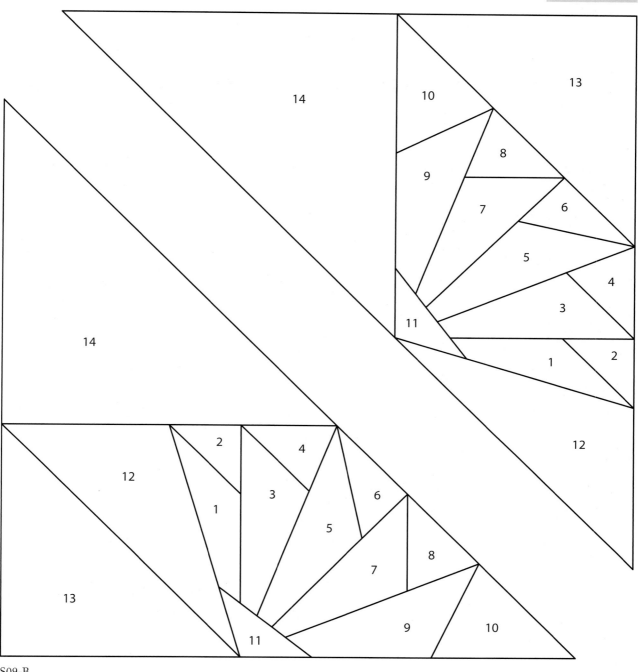

S09-A

14

10

13

8

9

7

6

5

4

3

11

1

2

12

14

12

2

4

3

1

5

6

13

7

8

9

10

11

S09-B

Block-front drawings

Make 4.

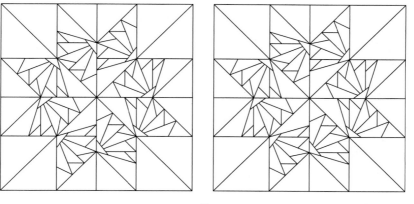

A

B

Georgia Star

80 PIECES

The following fabric cutting list is for one star block.

Fabric	Number of Pieces	Piece Dimensions	Piece Number	Block Section
Peach	8	1½″ × 2¾″	1	A, B
Light green	8	1½″ × 5″	4	A, B
Medium teal	8	1½″ × 6″	5	A, B
Dark blue	8	2″ × 2½″	2	A, B
	8	2″ × 3″	3	A, B
	16	1¼″ × 3″	6, 7	A, B
	8	2½″ × 2½″	8	A, B
Floral print	4	3¾″ × 3¾″ ◻	9	A, B
	4	4¾″ × 4¾″ ◻	10	A, B

S10-A

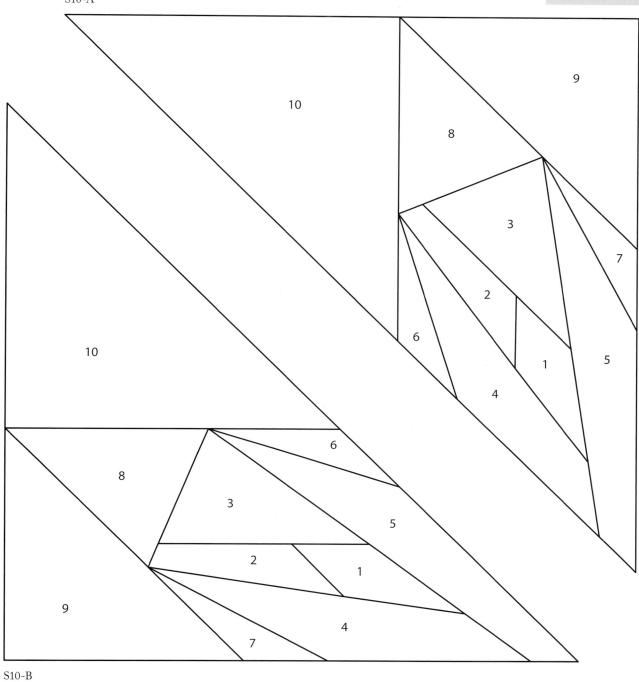

10

9

8

3

7

2

6

1

5

4

10

8

6

3

5

2

1

9

4

7

S10-B

Block-front drawings

Make 4.

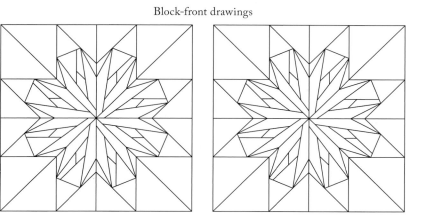

A

B

∽ STAR BLOCK 11 ∽
Hawaii Star

60 PIECES

The following fabric cutting list is for one star block.

Fabric	Number of Pieces	Piece Dimensions	Piece Number	Block Section
	4	1¼″ × 2¾″	2	B
	4	1¼″ × 4″	3	B
White	4	2″ × 4½″	1	A
	4	2″ × 6½″	8*	A, B
	4	1½″ × 4″	10*	A, B
Gold	4	1½″ × 3″	1	B
Purple	4	1½″ × 4″	4	B
Fuchsia	4	1¾″ × 5½″	5	B
Dark green	4	1¾″ × 5½″	3	A
Dark teal	4	1¾″ × 4″	2	A
Aqua	8	3¾″ × 3¾″ ◻	4, 5	A
			6, 7	B
Dark blue	4	2″ × 5½″	9*	A, B

Add these pieces after sections A and B are joined. See page 18.

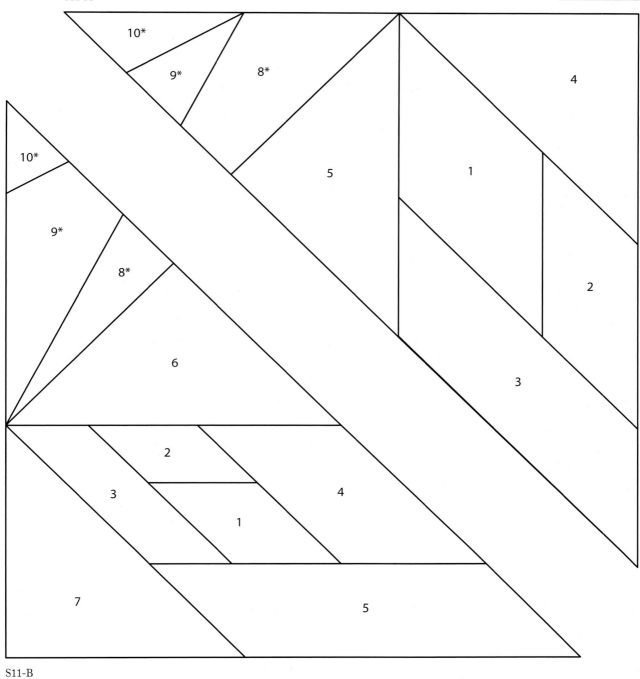

S11-A

10*

9*

8*

4

10*

5

1

9*

2

8*

6

3

2

3

4

1

7

5

S11-B

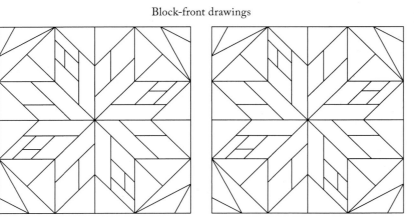

Block-front drawings

Make 4.

A

B

Hawaii Star

~ STAR BLOCK 12 ~
Idaho Star

64 PIECES

The following fabric cutting list is for one star block.

Fabric	Number of Pieces	Piece Dimensions	Piece Number	Block Section
Yellow	4	1¼″ × 2½″	1	A
Black	4	1¼″ × 2½″	2	A
	12	1¼″ × 3½″	3, 6, 7	A
	8	1″ × 3″	4, 5	B
	4	2½″ × 5½″	1	B
Light green	4	1¼″ × 4″	2	B
Light blue	4	1¼″ × 5″	3	B
Peach	4	2″ × 4″	4	A
Dark pink	4	2″ × 6″	5	A
Black print	4	3¾″ × 3¾″ ◻	9	A
			6	B
	4	4¾″ × 4¾″ ◻	8	A
			7	B

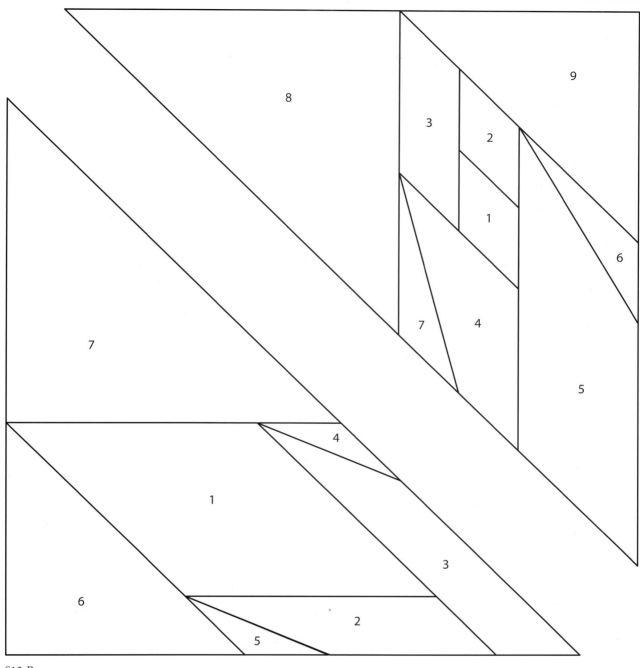

S12-A

8

9

3

2

1

7

4

6

5

7

4

1

3

6

2

5

S12-B

Block-front drawings

Make 4.

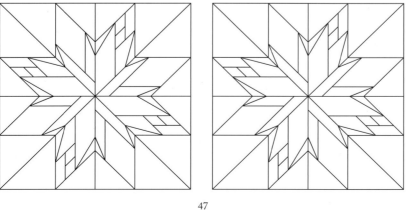

A

B

50 STATE STAR BLOCKS

Illinois Star

104 PIECES

The following fabric cutting list is for one star block.

Fabric	Number of Pieces	Piece Dimensions	Piece Number	Block Section
Dark red	8	1¼″ × 2¼″	1	A, B
Solid red	8	1¼″ × 3″	4	A, B
Red print	8	1¼″ × 4″	5	A, B
White	8	1¼″ × 2¼″	2	A, B
	8	1¼″ × 3½″	3	A, B
	32	1″ × 2½″	6, 7, 10, 11	A, B
Medium green	8	1¼″ × 4″	8	A, B
Dark green	8	1¼″ × 5″	9	A, B
Dark green print	4	3¾″ × 3¾″ ◩	12	A, B
	4	4¾″ × 4¾″ ◩	13	A, B

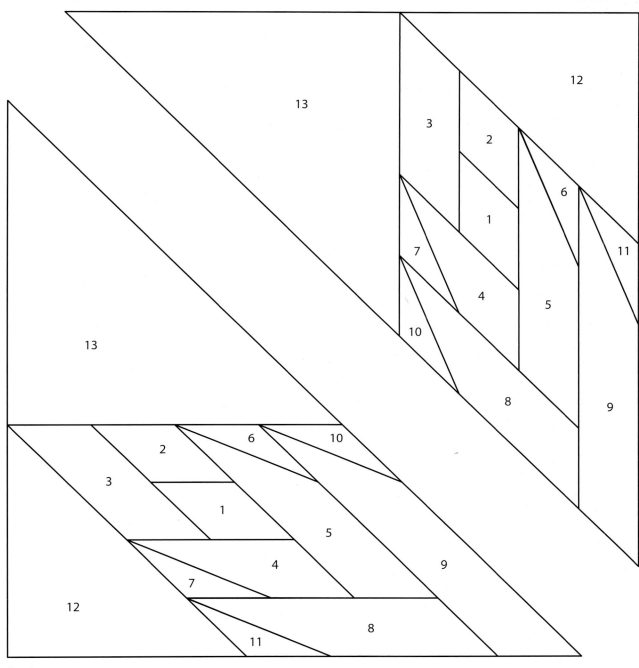

S13-A

S13-B

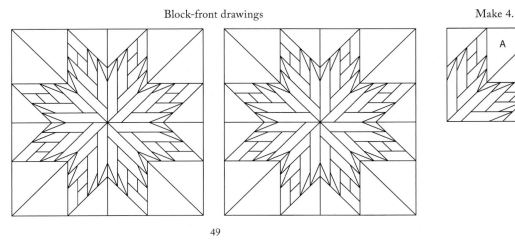

Block-front drawings

Make 4.

49

Illinois Star

STAR BLOCK 14

Indiana Star

64 PIECES

The following fabric cutting list is for one star block.

Fabric	Number of Pieces	Piece Dimensions	Piece Number	Block Section
Rust	4	2″ × 4½″	1	B
Orange	4	2″ × 4½″	4	B
Peach	4	2″ × 4½″	4	A
Yellow	4	2″ × 4½″	1	A
Green	16	2¼″ × 2¼″	2, 5	A, B
	16	1¼″ × 4″	6, 3	A, B
White and green print	4	3¾″ × 3¾″ ⧅	7	A, B
	4	4¾″ × 4¾″ ⧅	8	A, B

S14-A

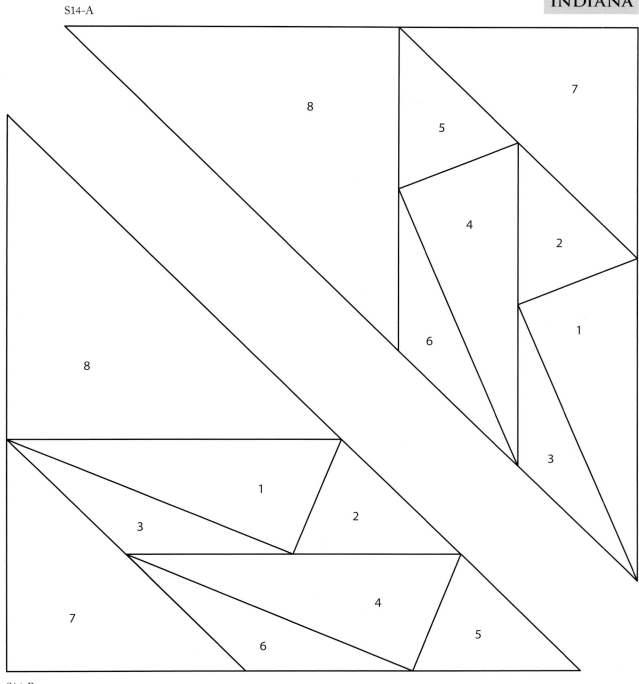

8

7

5

4

2

6

1

8

3

1

2

3

7

4

6

5

S14-B

Block-front drawings

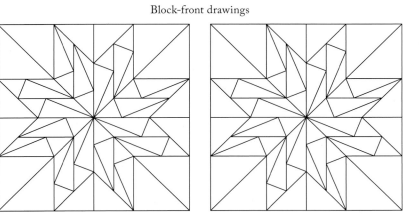

Make 4.

A

B

Indiana Star

STAR BLOCK 15

Iowa Star

112 PIECES

The following fabric cutting list is for one star block.

Fabric	Number of Pieces	Piece Dimensions	Piece Number	Block Section
Yellow	8	1¼″ × 2″	2	A, B
	8	1¼″ × 3″	3	A, B
	4	2½″ × 2½″ ⧄	13	A, B
Pink	8	1¼″ × 3½″	4	A, B
Orange print	8	1¼″ × 4″	5	A, B
Light green	4	1¼″ × 4″	8	B
	4	1¼″ × 5″	9	A
Dark green	4	1¼″ × 5″	9	B
	4	1¼″ × 4	8	A
Navy	8	1¼″ × 2″	1	A, B
	16	1″ × 2½″	6, 7	A, B
	8	2½″ × 2½″ ⧄	11, 14	A, B
Medium blue	8	1½″ × 5″	10	A, B
	8	3″ × 4½″	12	A, B

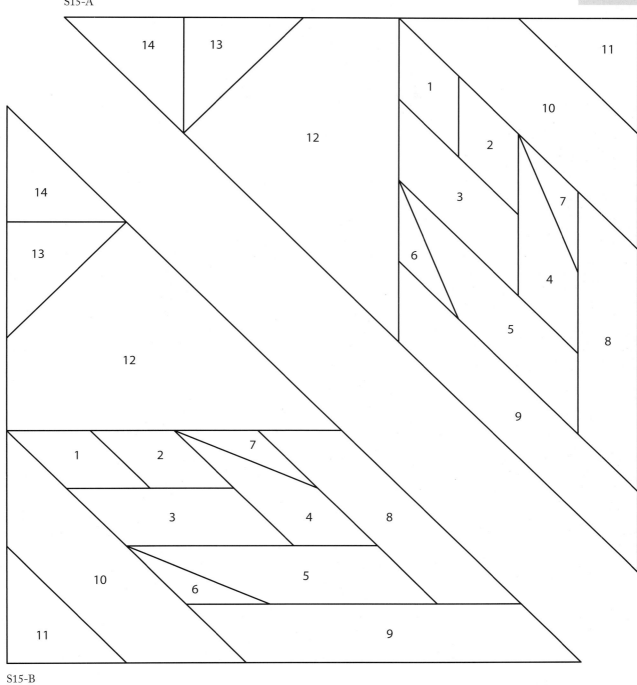

S15-A

14　13

14

13

11

12

1

10

2

3

7

6

4

5

8

12

9

1　2

7

3　4　8

10

5

11　6

9

S15-B

Block-front drawings

Make 4.

A

B

50 STATE STAR BLOCKS

STAR BLOCK 16
Kansas Star

40 PIECES

The following fabric cutting list is for one star block.

Fabric	Number of Pieces	Piece Dimensions	Piece Number	Block Section
Red	4	2″ × 6″	3	A
Yellow	4	2″ × 3¾″	2	A
Brown	4	2″ × 6″	3	B
Green	4	2″ × 3¾″	2	B
Floral print	8	2″ × 3¾″	1	A, B
	4	3¾″ × 3¾″ ◻	4	A, B
	4	4¾″ × 4¾″ ◻	5	A, B

S16-A

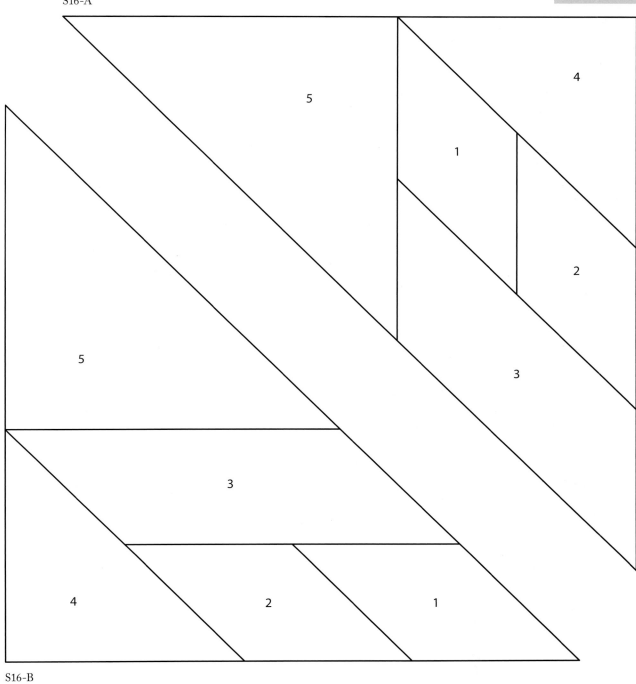

5

4

1

2

3

5

3

4

2

1

S16-B

Block-front drawings

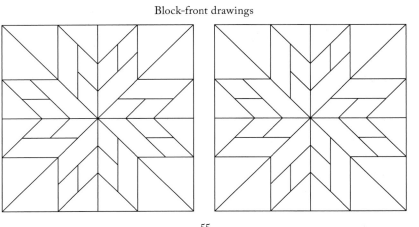

Make 4.

A

B

Kansas Star

✳

~ STAR BLOCK 17 ~

Kentucky Star

48 PIECES

> *The following fabric cutting list is for one star block.*

Fabric	Number of Pieces	Piece Dimensions	Piece Number	Block Section
Red print	8	3½″ × 4″	1	A, B
Red solid	4	1½″ × 3½″	3	A
Dark blue	4	1½″ × 4½″	4	A
Red stripe	4	1½″ × 3½″	3	B
Medium blue	4	1½″ × 4½″	4	B
White print	8	2½″ × 3½″	2	A, B
	4	3¾″ × 3¾″ ◹	5	A, B
	4	4¾″ × 4¾″ ◹	6	A, B

S17-A

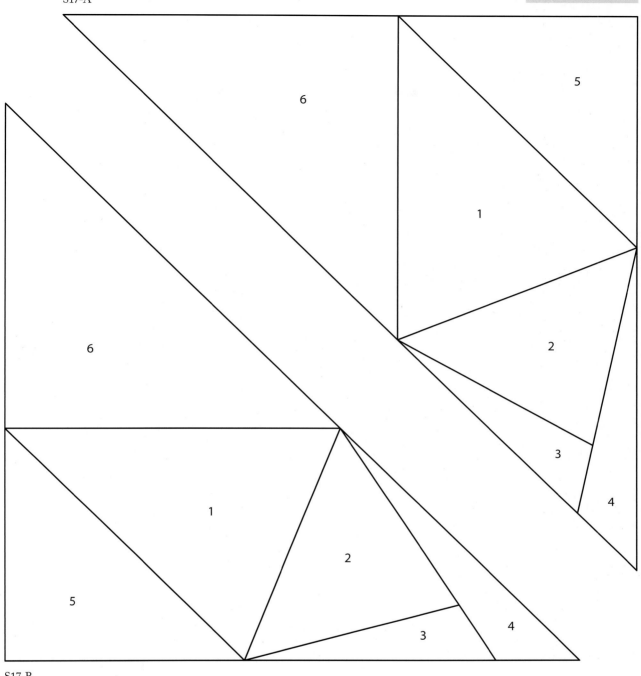

6

5

1

2

3

4

6

1

2

5

3

4

S17-B

Block-front drawings

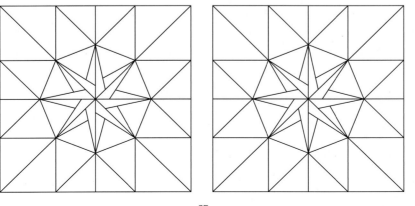

Make 4.

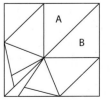

A

B

～ STAR BLOCK 18 ～
Louisiana Star

80 PIECES

The following fabric cutting list is for one star block.

Fabric	Number of Pieces	Piece Dimensions	Piece Number	Block Section
Pink print	8	3½″ × 4″	8	A, B
Pink stripe	8	1¼″ × 2″	1	A, B
Blue	8	1¼″ × 3″	4	A, B
Green	8	1¼″ × 4″	5	A, B
	32	1¼″ × 1¾″	2, 3, 6, 7	A, B
Light blue dot	4	3¾″ × 3¾″ ◻	9	A, B
	4	4¾″ × 4¾″ ◻	10	A, B

S18-A

10

9

8

6

2

3

7

1

4

10

5

7

2

4

8

1

3

5

9

6

S18-B

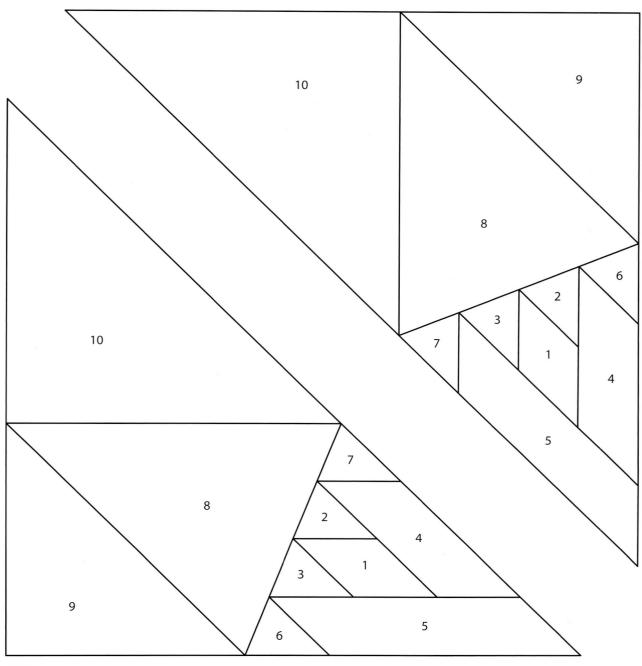

Block-front drawings

Make 4.

A

B

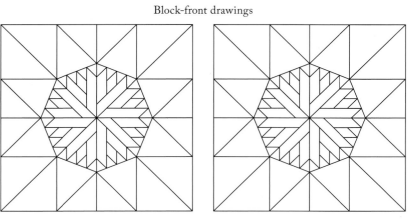

Louisiana Star

~ STAR BLOCK 19 ~

Maine Star

56 PIECES

> *The following fabric cutting list is for one star block.*

Fabric	Number of Pieces	Piece Dimensions	Piece Number	Block Section
Assorted solid colors	16	1¼″ × 3″	2, 3	A, B
	16	1¼″ × 5″	4, 5	A, B
Black	8	2″ × 4″	1	A, B
	4	3¾″ × 3¾″ ◻	6	A, B
	4	4¾″ × 4¾″ ◻	7	A, B

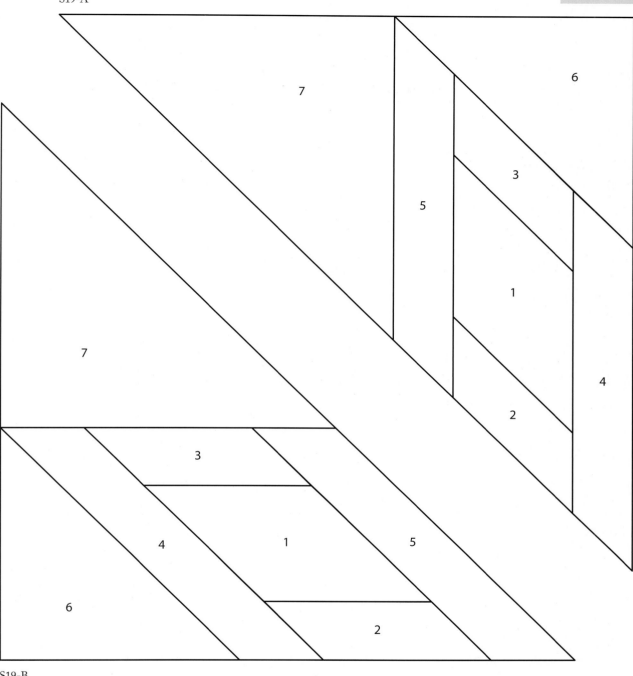

S19-A

7

6

5

3

1

2

4

7

3

4

1

5

6

2

S19-B

Block-front drawings

Make 4.

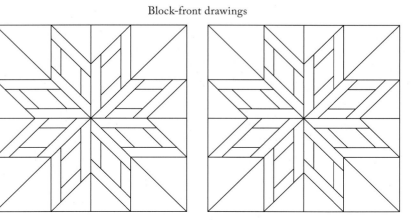

A

B

61

Maine Star

~ STAR BLOCK 20 ~
# Maryland Star

56 PIECES

The following fabric cutting list is for one star block.

Fabric	Number of Pieces	Piece Dimensions	Piece Number	Block Section
Yellow	8	2″ × 4″	1	A, B
	16	1¼″ × 3¾″	4, 5	A, B
Medium teal	4	2″ × 3¾″	2	B
Dark teal	4	2″ × 5½″	3	B
Medium purple	4	2″ × 3¾″	2	A
Dark purple	4	2″ × 5½″	3	A
Multi-color print	4	3¾″ × 3¾″ ◨	6	A, B
	4	4¾″ × 4¾″ ◨	7	A, B

S20-A

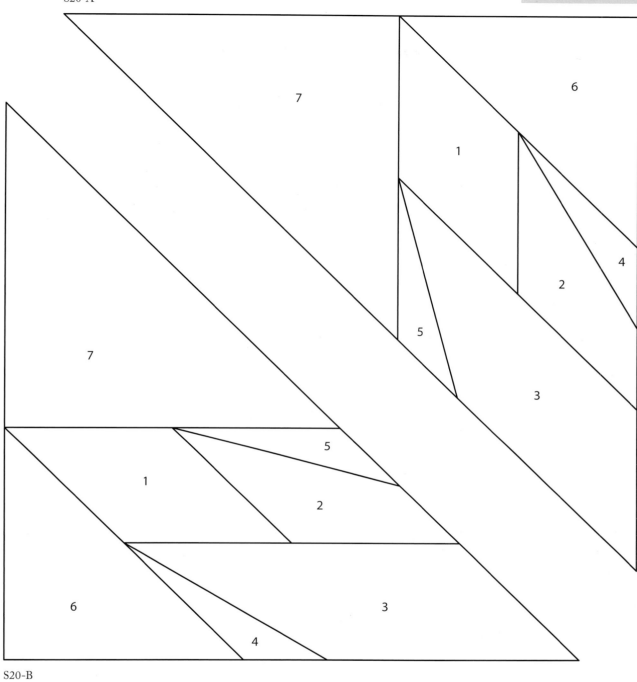

7

6

1

4

2

5

3

7

5

1

2

6

3

4

S20-B

Block-front drawings

Make 4.

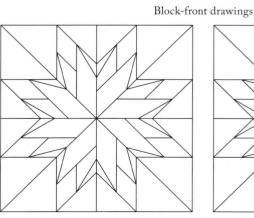

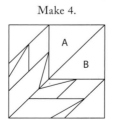

A

B

Maryland Star

⌒ STAR BLOCK 21 ⌒

Massachusetts Star

56 PIECES

The following fabric cutting list is for one star block.

Fabric	Number of Pieces	Piece Dimensions	Piece Number	Block Section
Black	8	2¾″ × 3″	3	A, B
Gold	16	1¼″ × 4″	2, 4	A, B
White	8	1¼″ × 5″	5	A, B
	8	2½″ × 2½″	1	A, B
Grey print	4	3¾″ × 3¾″ ◺	6	A, B
	4	4¾″ × 4¾″ ◺	7	A, B

S21-A

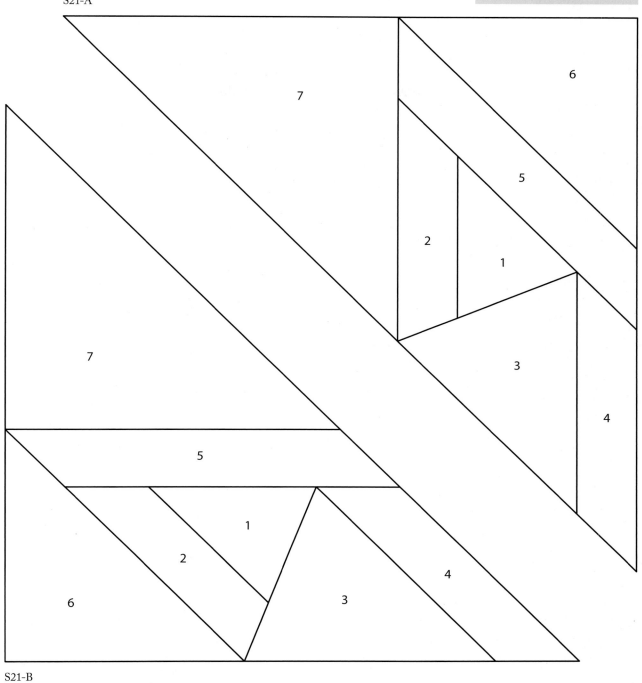

7

6

5

2

1

3

4

7

5

1

2

4

6

3

S21-B

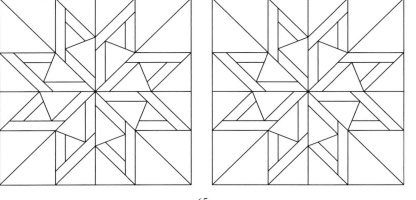

Block-front drawings

Make 4.

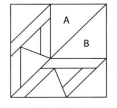

A

B

Massachusetts Star

✳

~ STAR BLOCK 22 ~
# Michigan Star

128 PIECES

The following fabric cutting list is for one star block.

Fabric	Number of Pieces	Piece Dimensions	Piece Number	Block Section
Light green	8	1½″ × 5″	14	A, B
Medium green	8	1½″ × 5″	13	A, B
Yellow	8	1¼″ × 2½″	1	A, B
Medium teal	8	1¼″ × 2½″	4	A, B
Light teal	8	1¼″ × 2½″	7	A, B
Blue	8	1¼″ × 2½″	10	A, B
Black	32	1¼″ × 2½″	3, 5, 8, 11	A, B
	32	1½″ × 1½″	2, 6, 9, 12	A, B
Black dot	4	3¾″ × 3¾″ �	15	A, B
	4	4¾″ × 4¾″ ◢	16	A, B

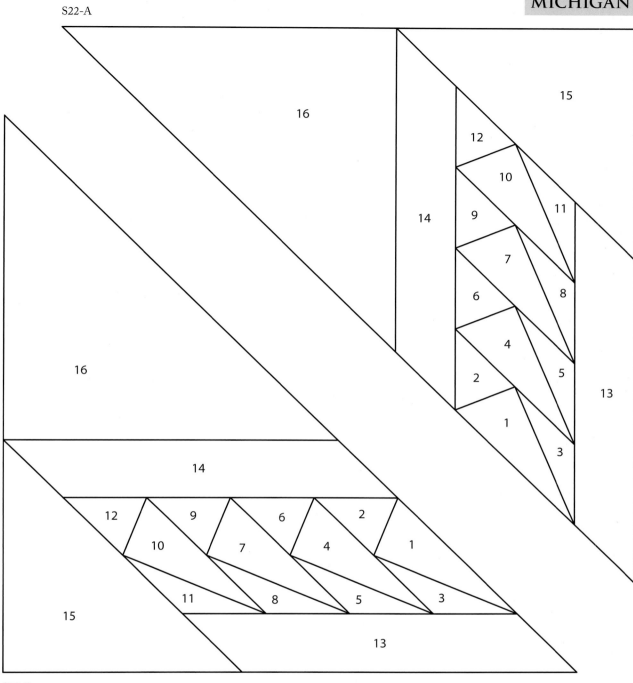

S22-A

16

15

12

10

14

9

11

7

6

8

4

5

2

13

1

3

S22-B

16

14

12

9

6

2

10

7

4

1

11

8

5

3

15

13

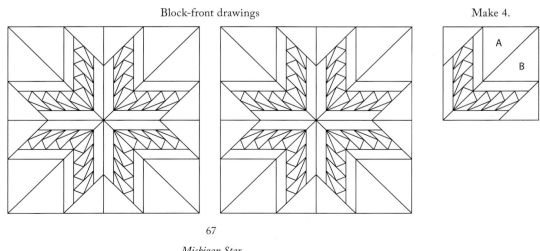

Block-front drawings

Make 4.

A

B

~ STAR BLOCK 23 ~

Minnesota Star

64 PIECES

The following fabric cutting list is for one star block.

Fabric	Number of Pieces	Piece Dimensions	Piece Number	Block Section
Floral	8	2½″ × 4″	1	A, B
	10	3¾″ × 3¾″ ◺	6, 7	A, B
			9*	A, B
Light pink	8	1½″ × 3½″	2	A, B
Medium pink	8	1½″ × 4½″	3	A, B
Orange print	8	1½″ × 4½″	4	A, B
	8	1½″ × 5½″	5	A, B
Green	4	1½″ × 6″	8*	A, B

*Add these pieces after sections A and B are joined. See page 18.

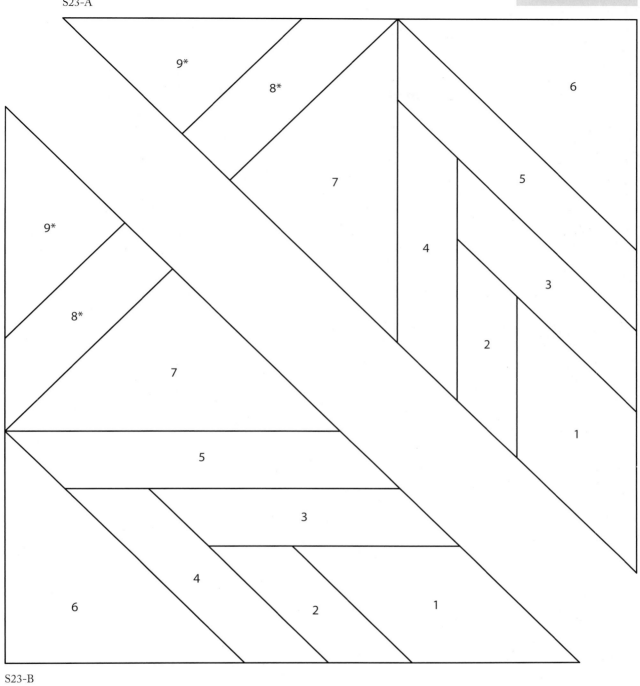

S23-A

9*

8*

6

7

5

4

3

2

1

9*

8*

7

5

3

4

2

1

6

S23-B

Block-front drawings

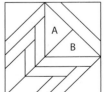

Make 4.

A

B

Minnesota Star

❊ STAR BLOCK 24 ❧
Mississippi Star

80 PIECES

The following fabric cutting list is for one star block.

Fabric	Number of Pieces	Piece Dimensions	Piece Number	Block Section
Yellow	8	1¼″ × 2¼″	2	A, B
	16	1¼″ × 3″	4, 5	A, B
	8	2″ × 2¼″	6	A, B
Medium teal	8	1¼″ × 4″	7	A, B
Blue	8	1¼″ × 5″	8	A, B
Medium pink	8	1½″ × 3″	1	A, B
Dark red	8	2″ × 3½″	3	A, B
Multi-color print	4	3¾″ × 3¾″ ◻	9	A, B
	4	4¾″ × 4¾″ ◻	10	A, B

S24-A

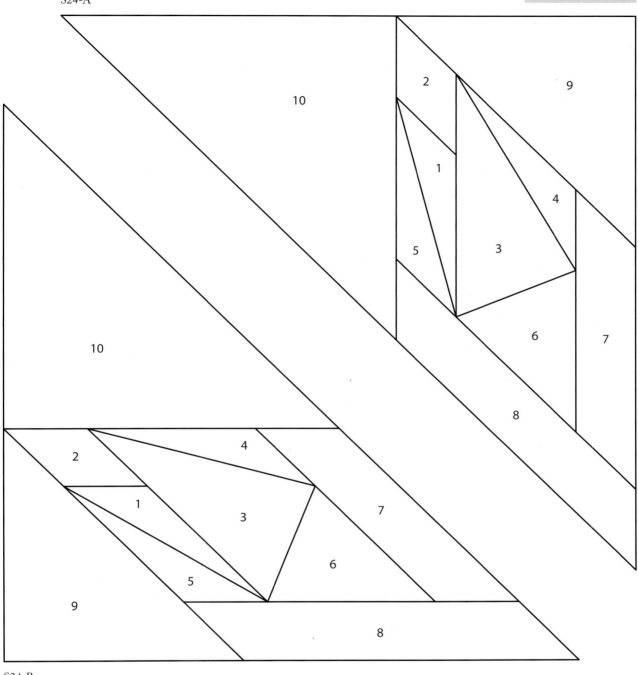

S24-B

Block-front drawings

Make 4.

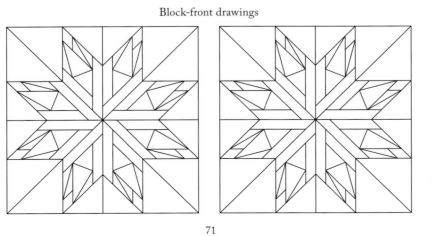

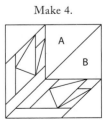

Mississippi Star

~ STAR BLOCK 25 ~

Missouri Star

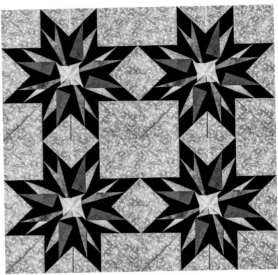

68 PIECES

The following fabric cutting list is for one star block.

Fabric	Number of Pieces	Piece Dimensions	Piece Number	Block Section
	8	2″ × 4″	1	A, B
	8	1½″ × 5″	4, 5	B
Black	8	1½″ × 4″	4, 5	A
	4	1½″ × 2″	6	A
	4	1½″ × 3″	2	B
Light green/blue	4	1½″ × 2½″	7	A
Dark green/blue	4	1½″ × 4¾″	3	B
Light green	2	2¼″ × 2¼″	6	B
Light pink	4	1¾″ × 4″	2	A
Dark pink	4	2″ × 4¼″	3	A
	4	3¾″ × 3¾″ ◻	8	A
			7	B
Grey			9	A
	4	4¾″ × 4¾″ ◻	8	B

S25-A

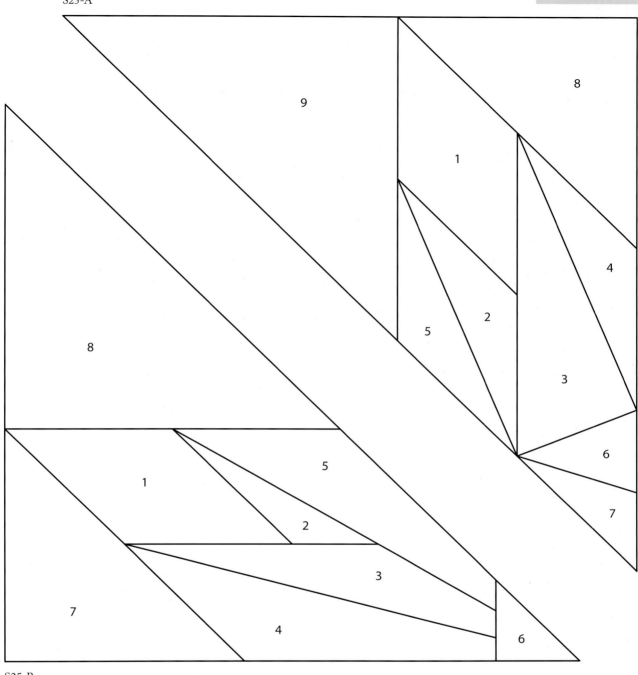

S25-B

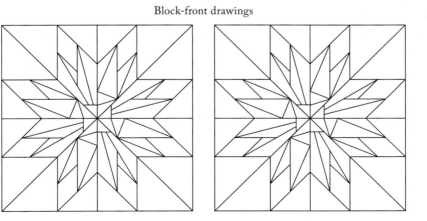

Block-front drawings

Make 4.

A

B

Missouri Star

~ STAR BLOCK 26 ~
Montana Star

56 PIECES

The following fabric cutting list is for one star block.

Fabric	Number of Pieces	Piece Dimensions	Piece Number	Block Section
Purple print	8	3″ × 4″	1	A, B
Yellow	8	1½″ × 3″	3	A, B
Medium blue	4	2½″ × 4½″	4	A
Medium green	4	2½″ × 4½″	4	B
White stripe	8	2½″ × 4½″	5	A, B
	8	1½″ × 3″	2	A, B
Light blue print	4	3¾″ × 3¾″ ◨	6	A, B
	4	4¾″ × 4¾″ ◨	7	A, B

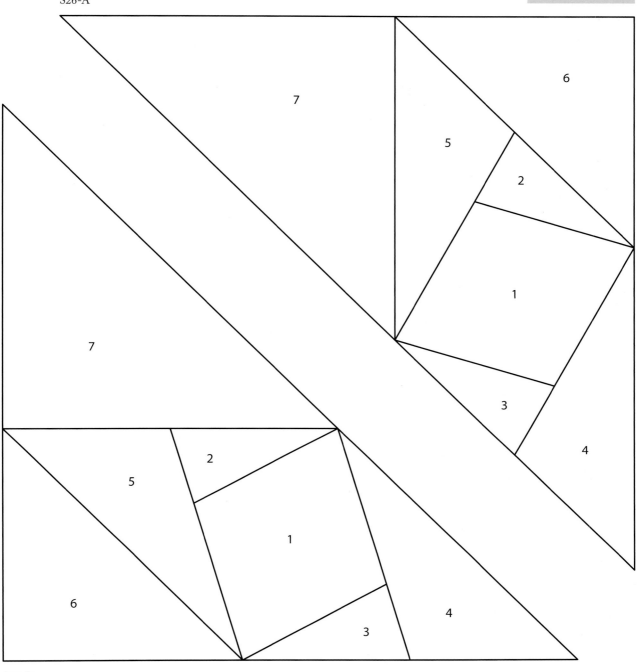

S26-A

S26-B

Block-front drawings

Make 4.

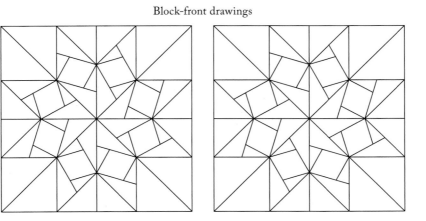

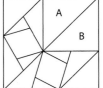

Montana Star

⌐ STAR BLOCK 27 ⌐
Nebraska Star

52 PIECES

> *The following fabric cutting list is for one star block.*

Fabric	Number of Pieces	Piece Dimensions	Piece Number	Block Section
Blue stripe	2	2¼″ × 2¼″ ◻	7*	A, B
	8	2″ × 4″	1	A, B
Dark teal	8	2″ × 7½″	4	A, B
White	16	2″ × 4″	2, 3	A, B
Medium green	2	3¾″ × 3¾″ ◻	5	A
	2	4¾″ × 4¾″ ◻	6	A
Light green	2	3¾″ × 3¾″ ◻	5	B
	2	4¾″ × 4¾″ ◻	6	B

*Add these pieces after A & B are joined. See page 18.

S27-A

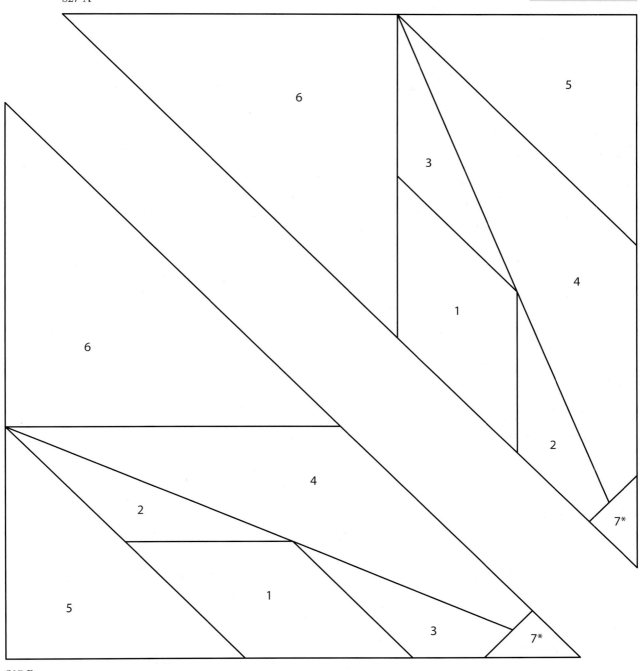

6

5

3

4

1

2

6

4

2

1

7*

2

5

3

7*

S27-B

Block-front drawings

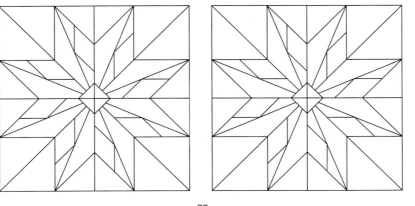

Make 4.

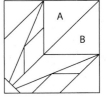

A

B

Nebraska Star

～ STAR BLOCK 28 ～
Nevada Star

60 PIECES

Fabric	Number of Pieces	Piece Dimensions	Piece Number	Block Section
Medium teal	8	2″ × 5½″	1	A, B
White print	16	1½″ × 5½″	2, 3	A, B
Gold	2	3¼″ × 3¼″	8*	A, B
Dark teal	8	2½″ × 2½″	4	A, B
Light green	8	2″ × 4½″	7	A, B
Pink	4	3¾″ × 3¾″ ◻	5	A, B
	8	2¼″ × 4½″	6	A, B

The following fabric cutting list is for one star block.

*Add these pieces after sections A and B are joined. See page 18.

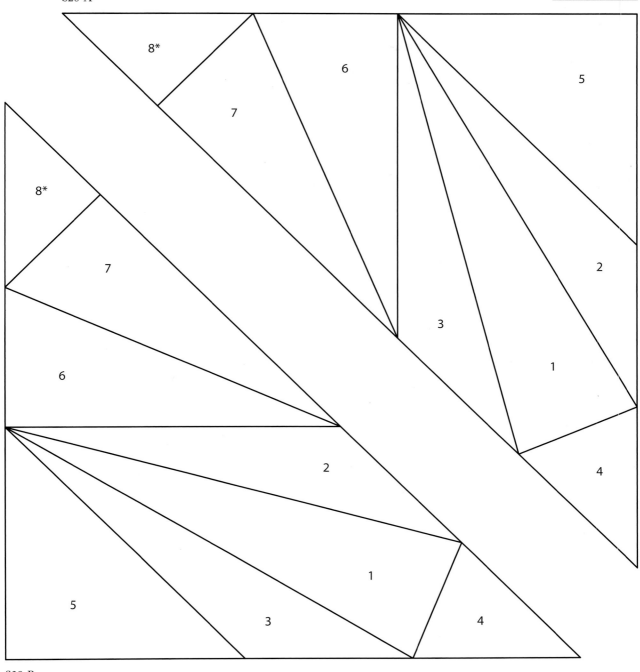

S28-A

8*

6

5

7

8*

7

3

2

6

1

2

1

4

5

3

4

S28-B

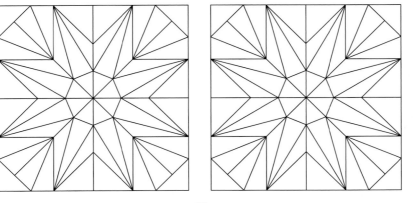

Block-front drawings

Make 4.

A

B

New Hampshire Star

96 PIECES

The following fabric cutting list is for one star block.

Fabric	Number of Pieces	Piece Dimensions	Piece Number	Block Section
Gold	4	1″ × 1½″	1	A
	8	1¼″ × 2″	2, 3	A
	8	1¼″ × 3½″	6, 7	A
Navy	24	1¼″ × 2½″	10, 11	A
			4, 5, 8, 9	B
	4	2″ × 4″	1	B
Light pink	4	2″ × 3″	4	A
Medium pink	4	2″ × 5″	5	A
Light purple	4	1¼″ × 3½″	2	B
Dark purple	4	1¼″ × 4″	3	B
Light teal	8	1¼″ × 4″	8	A
			6	B
Medium teal	8	1¼″ × 5″	9	A
			7	B
White print	4	3¾″ × 3¾″ ◻	12	A
			10	B
	4	4¾″ × 4¾″ ◻	13	A
			11	B

S29-A

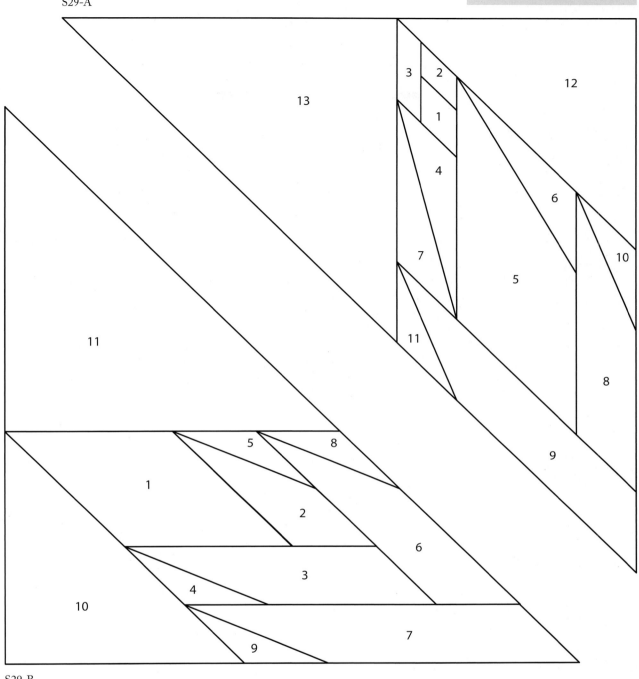

13

3   2

1

4

12

6

7

11

5

10

8

11

9

S29-B

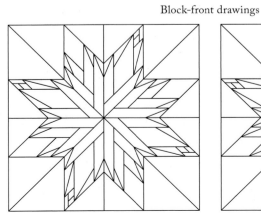

1

5   8

2

6

3

4

10

9

7

Block-front drawings

Make 4.

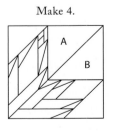

A

B

New Hampshire Star

～ STAR BLOCK 30 ～
New Jersey Star

72 PIECES

The following fabric cutting list is for one star block.

Fabric	Number of Pieces	Piece Dimensions	Piece Number	Block Section
Gold	8	2″ × 2″	1	A, B
Black	8	2½″ × 2½″ ◰	2, 3	A, B
	8	2½″ × 4″	6	A, B
Light blue	4	1¼″ × 2½″	4	A
Medium blue	4	2″ × 3½″	5	A
Coral	4	1¼″ × 2½″	4	B
Coral print	4	2″ × 3½″	5	B
Dark green	4	2½″ × 4½″	7	A
Light green	4	2½″ × 4½″	7	B
White	4	3¾″ × 3¾″ ◳	8	A, B
	4	4¾″ × 4¾″ ◳	9	A, B

S30-A

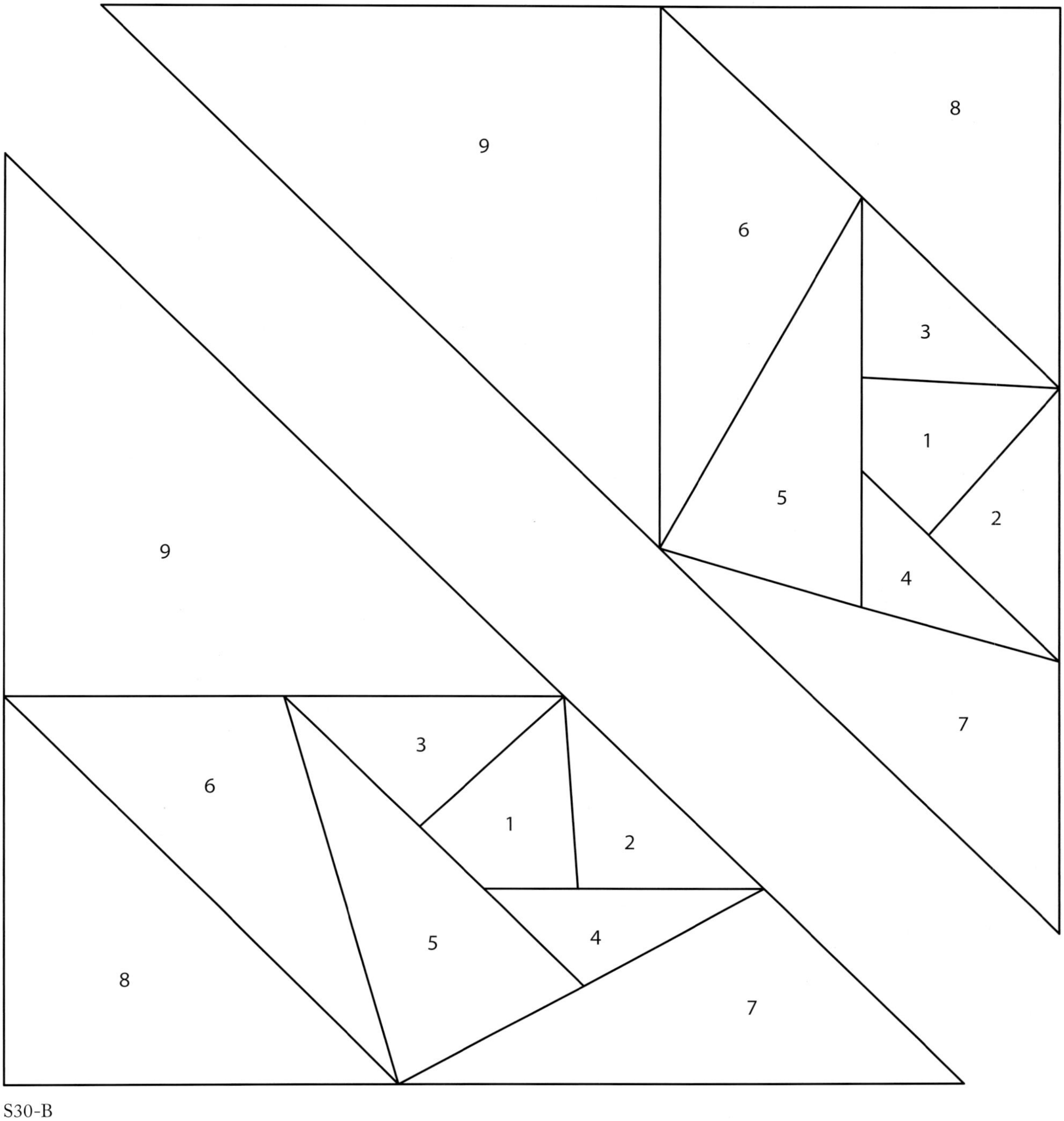

9

8

6

3

1

5

2

4

7

9

3

6

1

2

5

4

8

7

S30-B

Block-front drawings

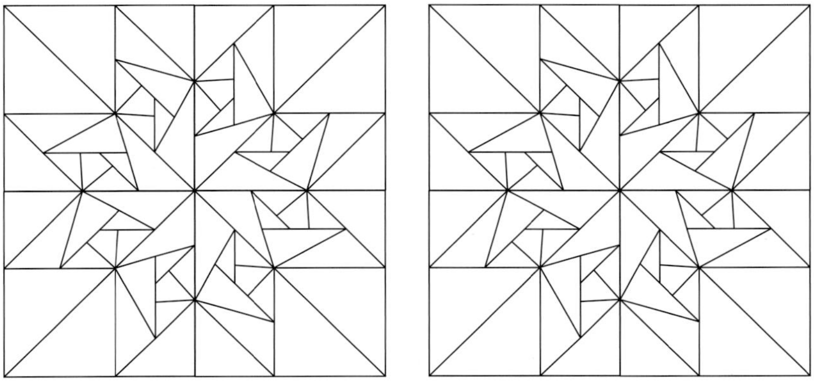

Make 4.

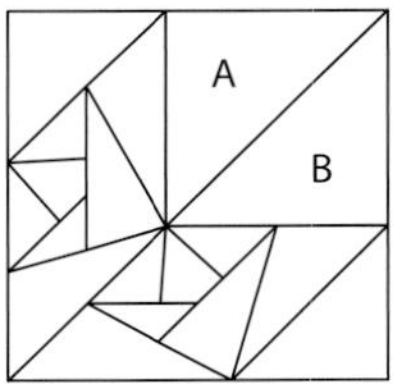

A

B

New Jersey Star

⌐ STAR BLOCK 31 ⌐
New Mexico Star

72 PIECES

The following fabric cutting list is for one star block.

Fabric	Number of Pieces	Piece Dimensions	Piece Number	Block Section
Coral	8	2″ × 3½″	1	A, B
Yellow/green print	16	2″ × 3″	2, 3	A, B
	8	3¼″ × 3¼″ ◻	6, 7	A, B
Red print	16	1″ × 3½″	4, 5	A, B
Teal	4	3¾″ × 3¾″ ◻	8	A, B
	4	4¾″ × 4¾″ ◻	9	A, B

S31-A

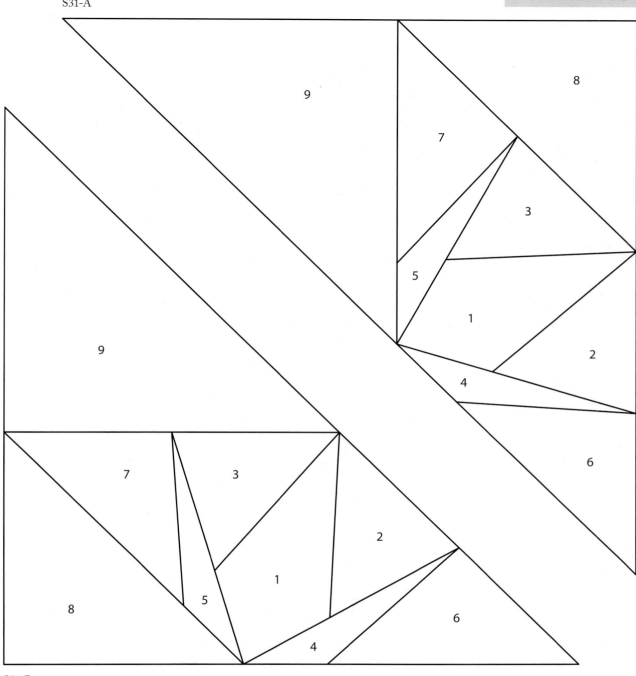

9

8

7

3

5

1

2

4

9

6

7

3

2

1

5

8

6

4

S31-B

Block-front drawings

Make 4.

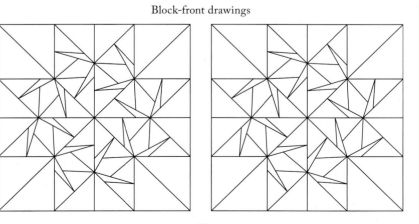

A

B

New Mexico Star

~ STAR BLOCK 32 ~

New York Star

64 PIECES

The following fabric cutting list is for one star block.

Fabric	Number of Pieces	Piece Dimensions	Piece Number	Block Section
Print fabric	8	2½″ × 4½″	1	A, B
Pink print	16	2″ × 3″	2, 3	A, B
	8	2¼″ × 3¼	5	A, B
Teal	8	1½″ × 4″	6	A, B
Black/white stripe	8	1½″ × 4″	4	A, B
Black	4	3¾″ × 3¾″ ◻	7	A, B
	4	4¾″ × 4¾″ ◻	8	A, B

S32-A

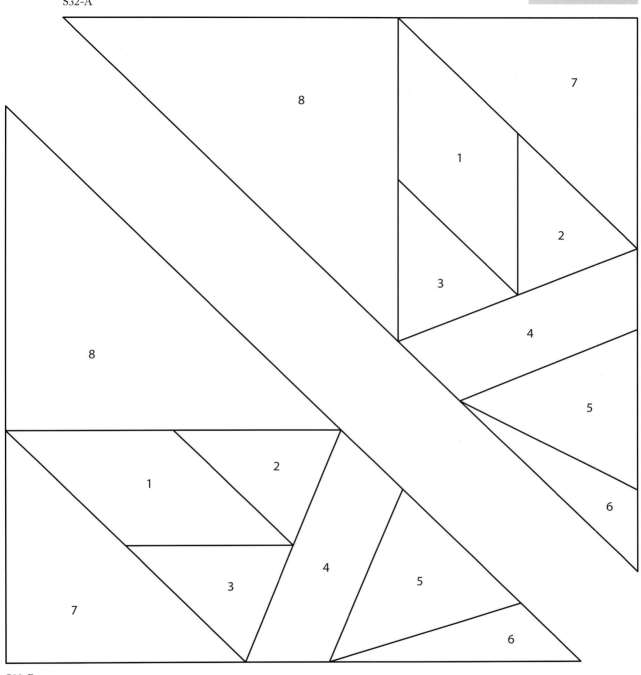

S32-B

Block-front drawings

Make 4.

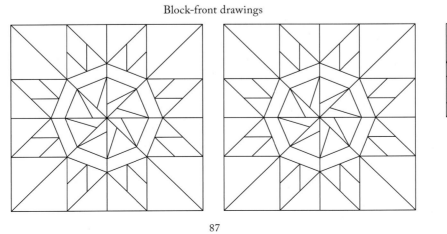

New York Star

50 STATE STAR BLOCKS

~ STAR BLOCK 33 ~
North Carolina Star

72 PIECES

The following fabric cutting list is for one star block.

Fabric	Number of Pieces	Piece Dimensions	Piece Number	Block Section
Light peach	8	2″ × 2½″	1	A, B
	16	1½″ × 2″	4, 5	A, B
Orange solid	4	1¼″ × 4″	3	A
Dark green	4	1¼″ × 3″	2	A
Medium green	4	1¼″ × 4″	3	B
Orange print	4	1¼″ × 3″	2	B
Light green	8	1½″ × 4″	6	A, B
Orange swirl print	8	3″ × 3″	7	A, B
Dark brown	4	3¾″ × 3¾″ ◨	8	A, B
	4	4¾″ × 4¾″ ◨	9	A, B

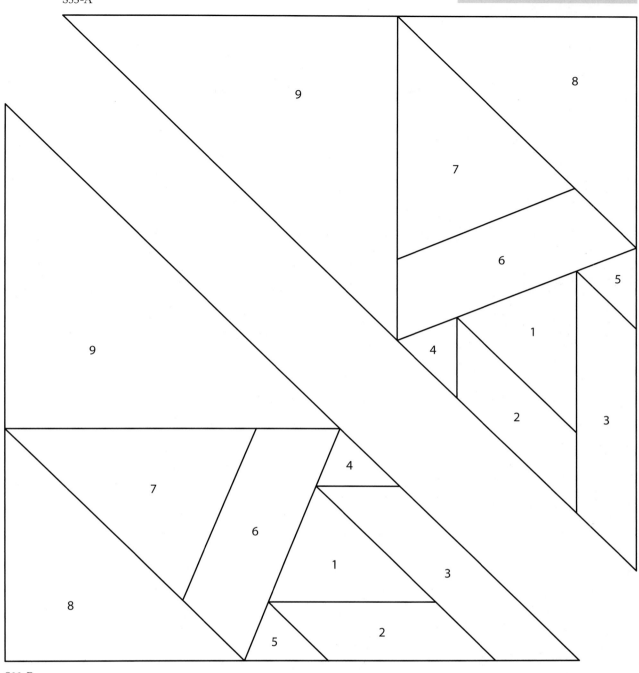

S33-A

S33-B

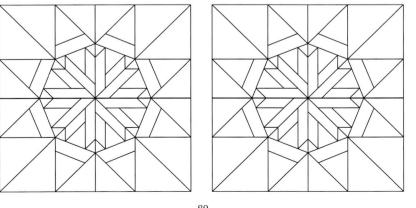

Block-front drawings

Make 4.

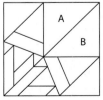

89

North Carolina Star

~ STAR BLOCK 34 ~
# North Dakota Star

88 PIECES

The following fabric cutting list is for one star block.

Fabric	Number of Pieces	Piece Dimensions	Piece Number	Block Section
White print	8	2″ × 3¾″	1	A, B
	24	1¼″ × 2½″	4, 5	B
			8, 9	A, B
	8	1¼″ × 3½″	4, 5	A
Green #1	4	1¼″ × 3¼″	2	B
Green #2	4	1¼″ × 4″	3	B
Green #3	8	1¼″ × 4″	6	A, B
Green #4	8	1¼″ × 5″	7	A, B
Solid red	4	1¼″ × 3¼″	2	A
Red print	4	1¼″ × 4″	3	A
Floral print	4	3¾″ × 3¾″ �◻	10	A, B
	4	4¾″ × 4¾″ ◻	11	A, B

S34-A

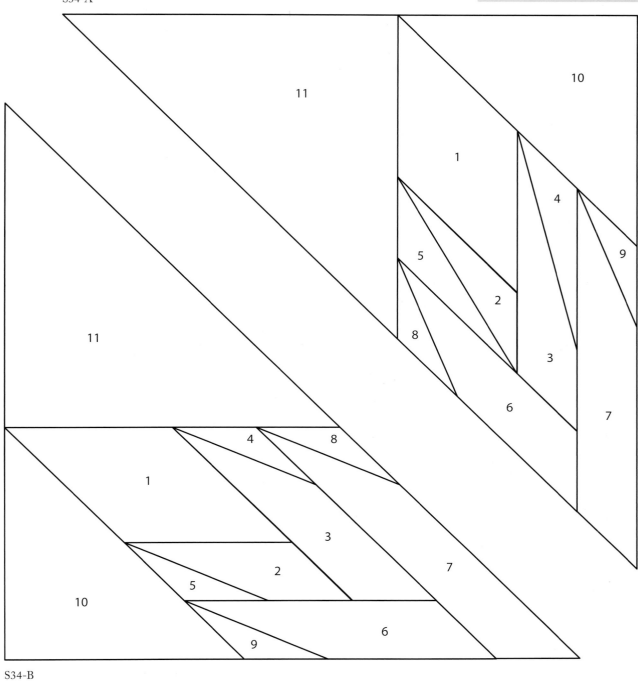

11

10

1

4

9

5

2

11

8

3

6

7

S34-B

1

4

8

3

2

7

5

10

9

6

Block-front drawings

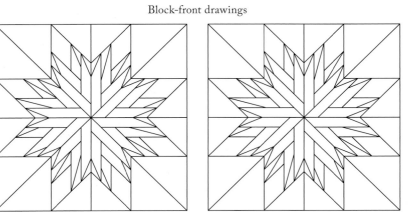

Make 4.

A

B

North Dakota Star

~ STAR BLOCK 35 ~
# Ohio Star

72 PIECES

The following fabric cutting list is for one star block.

Fabric	Number of Pieces	Piece Dimensions	Piece Number	Block Section
	8	2″ × 4″	1	A, B
Dark pink	8	1¼″ × 4″	4	A, B
	8	1¼″ × 5″	5	A, B
	8	1¼″ × 3¼″	2	A, B
	8	1¼″ × 4″	3	A, B
White	16	1¼″ × 2¾″	6, 7	A, B
	4	3¾″ × 3¾″ ◻	8	A, B
	4	4¾″ × 4¾″ ◻	9	A, B

S35-A

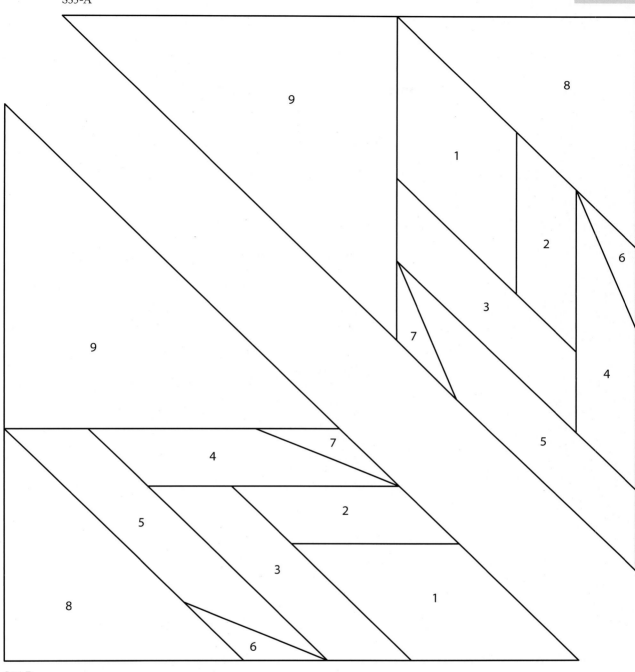

9

8

1

2

6

3

7

4

5

9

7

4

2

5

3

1

8

6

S35-B

Block-front drawings

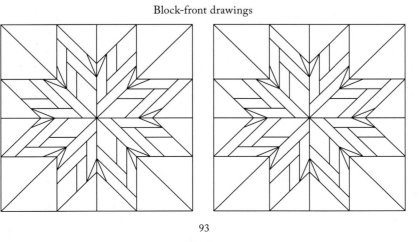

Make 4.

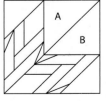

A

B

Ohio Star

50 STATE STAR BLOCKS

～ STAR BLOCK 36 ～
Oklahoma Star

128 PIECES

The following fabric cutting list is for one star block.

Fabric	Number of Pieces	Piece Dimensions	Piece Number	Block Section
Teal	16	1¼″ × 5″	13, 14	A, B
	8	1¼″ × 2½″	1	A, B
Medium dark blue	8	1¼″ × 2½″	4	A, B
Medium blue	8	1¼″ × 2½″	7	A, B
Light blue	8	1¼″ × 2½″	10	A, B
Black	32	1¼″ × 2¼″	3, 6, 9, 12	A, B
	32	1½″ × 1½″	2, 5, 8, 11	A, B
	4	3¾″ × 3¾″ ◻	15	A, B
	4	4¾″ × 4¾″ ◻	16	A, B

S36-A

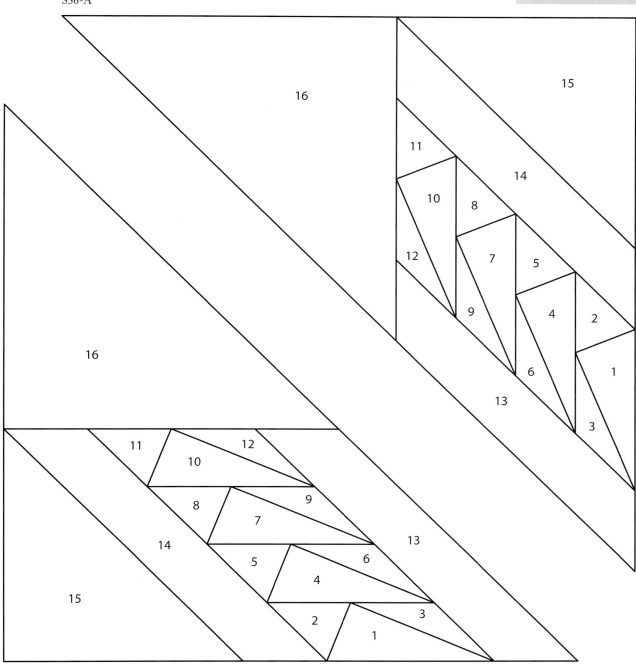

16

15

11

10

8

14

12

7

5

9

4

2

6

1

13

3

16

11

12

10

8

9

7

14

13

5

6

4

3

15

2

1

S36-B

Block-front drawings

Make 4.

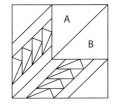

A

B

～ STAR BLOCK 37 ～
Oregon Star

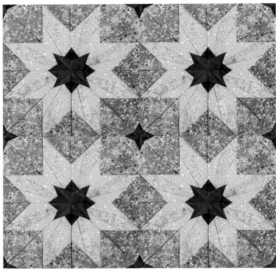

64 PIECES

The following fabric cutting list is for one star block.

Fabric	Number of Pieces	Piece Dimensions	Piece Number	Block Section
Light green print	8	2″ × 6″	1	A, B
Yellow	16	1½″ × 4½″	2, 3	A, B
Dark blue	4	1½″ × 2¼″	8	B
	8	1¼″ × 2″	4	A, B
Dark pink	4	1¼″ × 2¼″	8	A
	8	1½″ × 3¼″	5	A, B
Medium blue print	4	3¾″ × 3¾″ ◩	6	A, B
	4	4¾″ × 4¾″ ◩	7	A, B

S37-A

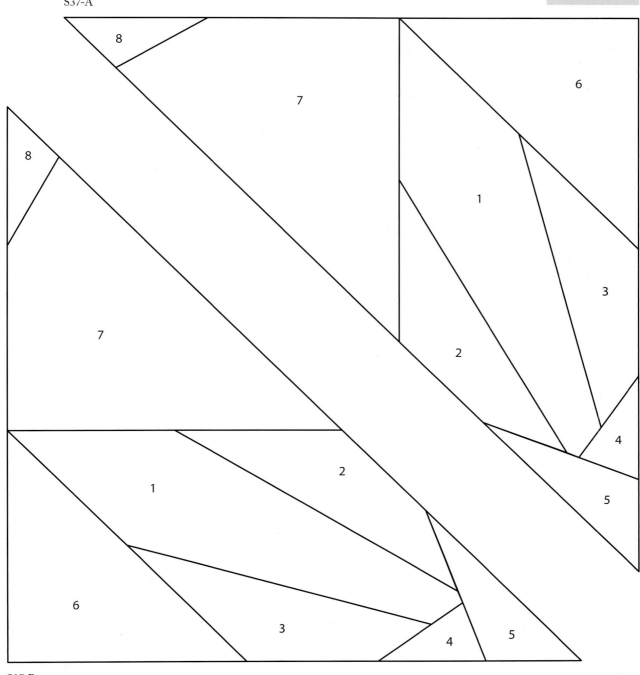

8

7

6

8

1

7

3

2

2

1

4

2

6

3

5

4

5

S37-B

Block-front drawings

Make 4.

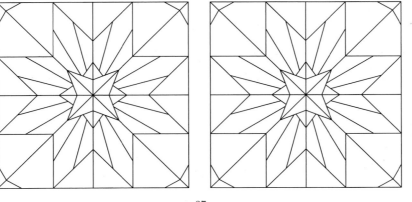

A

B

Oregon Star

~ STAR BLOCK 38 ~
# Pennsylvania Star

64 PIECES

The following fabric cutting list is for one star block.

Fabric	Number of Pieces	Piece Dimensions	Piece Number	Block Section
Blue	8	2″ × 4½″	1	A, B
Rose	8	2″ × 4½″	4	A, B
Gold	16	1½″ × 2½″	2, 5	A, B
	16	1¼″ × 3½″	3, 6	A, B
White print	4	3¾″ × 3¾″ ◹	7	A, B
	4	4¾″ × 4¾″ ◹	8	A, B

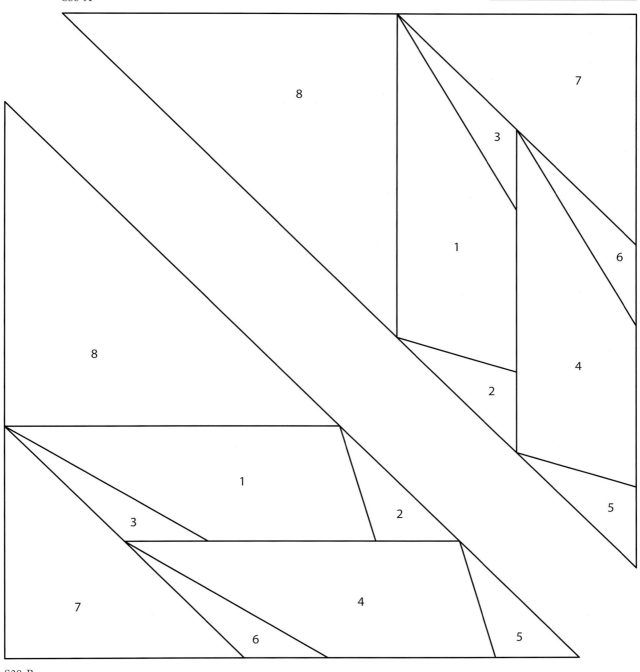

S38-A

8

7

3

1

2

6

4

5

S38-B

8

1

2

3

7

4

6

5

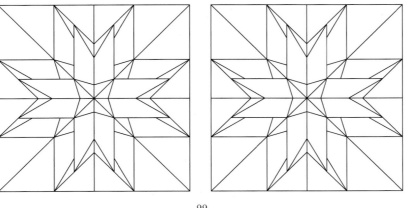

Block-front drawings

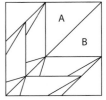

Make 4.

A

B

Pennsylvania Star

~ STAR BLOCK 39 ~
# Rhode Island Star

64 PIECES

The following fabric cutting list is for one star block.

Fabric	Number of Pieces	Piece Dimensions	Piece Number	Block Section
Coral/gold print	8	2″ × 5″	1	A, B
Dark blue	8	2″ × 5″	4	A, B
Light gold	4	2″ × 2½″	5	A
Medium gold	4	2″ × 2½″	5	B
Medium blue print	16	1¼″ × 3½″	3, 6	A, B
	8	2″ × 2½″	2	A, B
	4	3¾″ × 3¾″ ◻	7	A, B
	4	4¾″ × 4¾″ ◻	8	A, B

S39-A

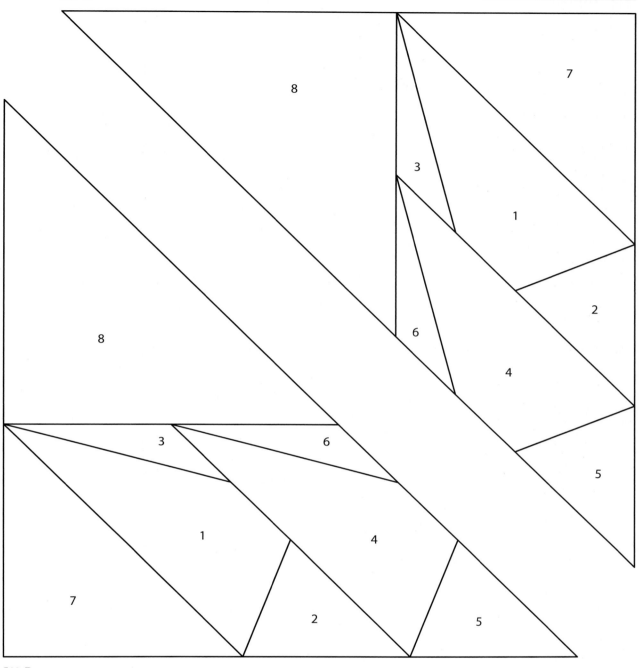

8

7

8

3

1

6

2

4

3

6

5

1

4

7

2

5

S29-B

Block-front drawings

Make 4.

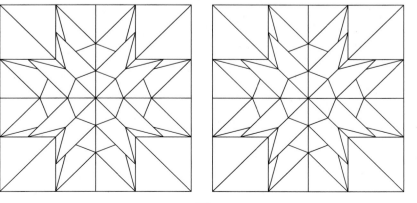

A

B

Rhode Island Star

South Carolina Star

120 PIECES

The following fabric cutting list is for one star block.

Fabric	Number of Pieces	Piece Dimensions	Piece Number	Block Section
Dark teal	8	1¼″ × 5″	12	A, B
	8	1¼″ × 2¼″	6	A, B
Medium teal	8	1¼″ × 5″	10	A, B
	8	1¼″ × 2¼″	4	A, B
Medium-light teal	8	1¼″ × 5″	8	A, B
	8	1¼″ × 2¼″	2	A, B
Black print	56	1¼″ × 2¼″	1, 3,5, 7, 9, 11,13	A, B
	4	3¾″ × 3¾″ ◩	14	A, B
	4	4¾″ × 4¾″ ◩	15	A, B

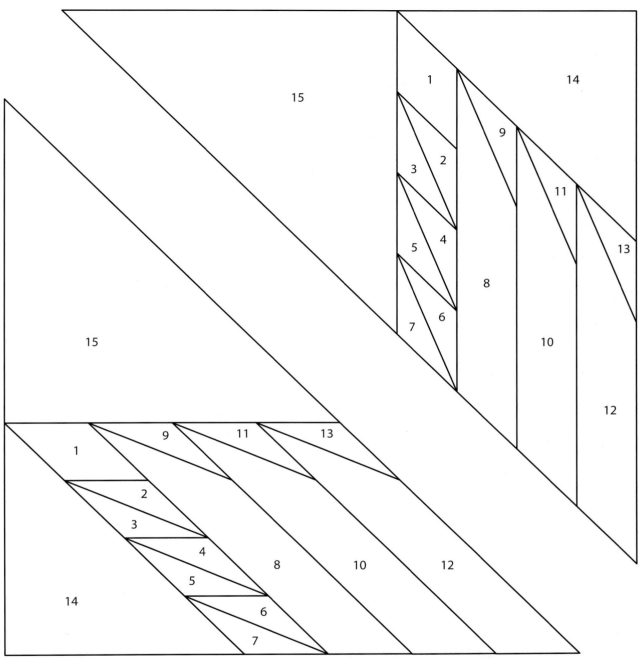

S40-A

S40-B

Block-front drawings

Make 4.

South Carolina Star

~ STAR BLOCK 41 ~
# South Dakota Star

100 PIECES

The following fabric cutting list is for one star block.

Fabric	Number of Pieces	Piece Dimensions	Piece Number	Block Section
Purple	8	2″ × 4″	1	A, B
	32	1¼″ × 3″	4, 5, 8, 9	A, B
	2	2½″ × 2½″ ◻	13*	A, B
Green #1	8	1¼″ × 4¼″	3	A, B
	8	1½″ × 4″	12	A, B
Green #2	8	1¼″ × 5¼″	7	A, B
Green #3	8	1¼″ × 3¼″	2	A, B
Green #4	8	1¼″ × 4½″	6	A, B
Blue print	4	3¾″ × 3¾″ ◻	10	A, B
	8	3″ × 4½″	11	A, B

*Add these pieces after sections A and B are joined. See page 18.

S41-A

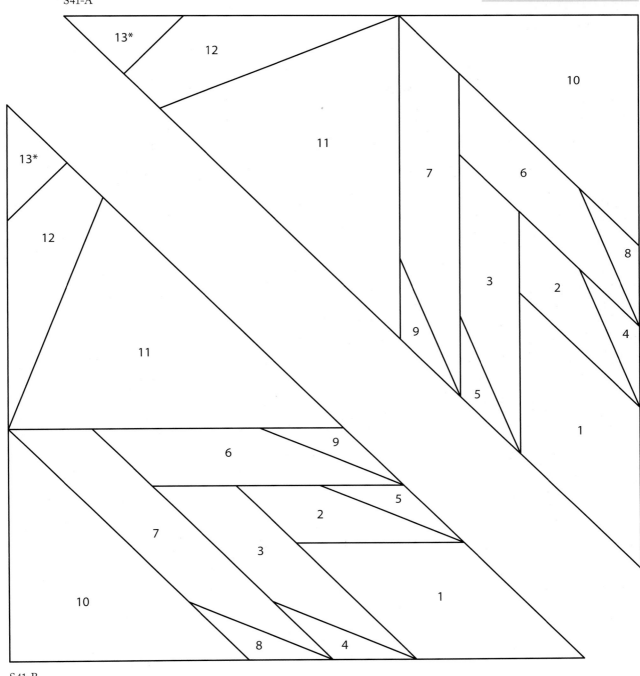

13*

12

10

13*

11

12

7

6

11

3

9

2

8

5

4

9

6

1

5

2

7

3

10

1

8

4

S41-B

Block-front drawings

Make 4.

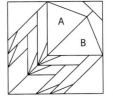

A

B

South Dakota Star

～ STAR BLOCK 42 ～

Tennessee Star

64 PIECES

The following fabric cutting list is for one star block.

Fabric	Number of Pieces	Piece Dimensions	Piece Number	Block Section
Medium pink	8	1½″ × 2½″	2	A, B
	4	1½″ × 3½″	7	A
Medium dark pink	8	2½″ × 4″	3	A, B
Medium teal	8	1¼″ × 3½″	5	A, B
	4	1½″ × 3½″	7	B
Light teal	8	1¼″ × 2½″	4	A, B
Blue print	8	4″ × 4″	1	A, B
	4	3¾″ × 3¾″ ◺	8	A, B
	4	4¾″ × 4¾″ ◺	6	A, B

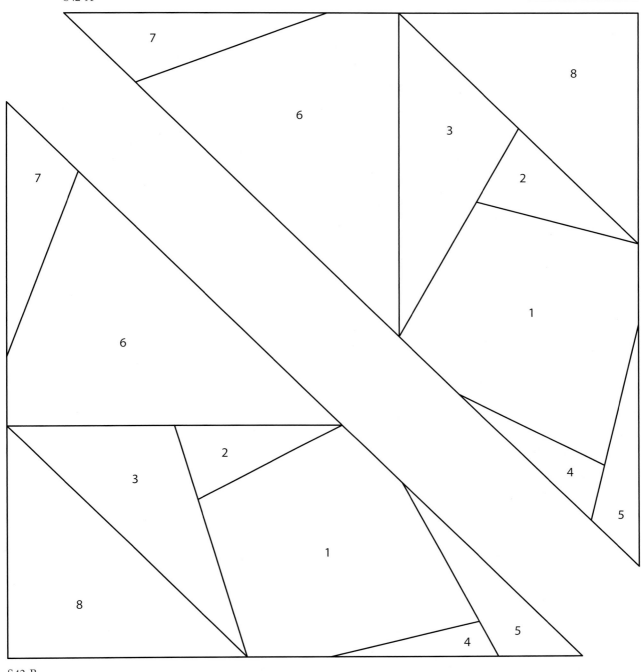

S42-A

7

6

8

3

2

7

1

6

2

3

1

8

4

5

4

5

S42-B

Block-front drawings

Make 4.

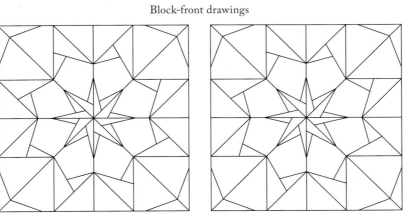

A

B

Tennessee Star

50 STATE STAR BLOCKS

✳

❦ STAR BLOCK 43 ❧

Texas Star

68 PIECES

The following fabric cutting list is for one star block.

Fabric	Number of Pieces	Piece Dimensions	Piece Number	Block Section
Red	8	1¼″ × 4″	2	A, B
Black	4	1½″ × 6″	8*	A, B
	2	3″ × 3″ ◻	10*	A, B
Teal	8	1¼″ × 5″	3	A, B
	4	1¼″ × 4″	9*	A, B
Blue print	8	2½″ × 5¼″	1	A, B
	16	1¼″ × 2½″	4, 5	A, B
	8	3¾″ × 3¾″ ◻	6, 7	A, B

*Add these pieces after sections A and B are joined. See page 18.

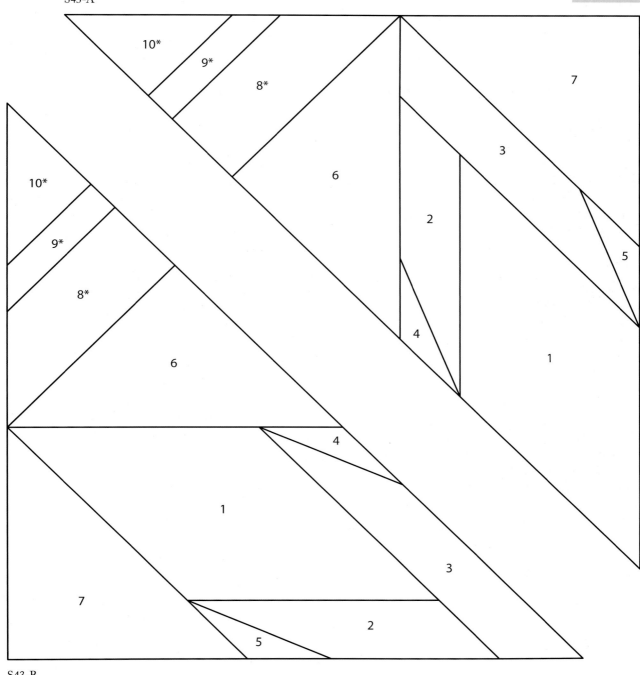

S43-A

10*

9*

8*

7

10*

9*

8*

6

3

2

4

5

6

4

1

1

3

7

2

5

S43-B

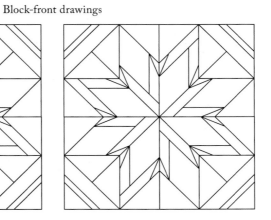

Block-front drawings

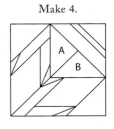

Make 4.

A

B

Texas Star

~ STAR BLOCK 44 ~

Utah Star

64 PIECES

The following fabric cutting list is for one star block.

Fabric	Number of Pieces	Piece Dimensions	Piece Number	Block Section
Gold	4	1½″ × 3¼″	2	B
Royal blue	4	2″ × 4″	1	A
Teal print	4	1½″ × 4¼″	4	B
	4	1½″ × 5″	5	B
	4	2″ × 2″	4	A
	4	3½″ × 4½″	5	A
Yellow	4	1½″ × 4¼″	3	B
	4	2¼″ × 2¼″ ◻	7	A, B
Red	4	2″ × 4″	1	B
	8	1½″ × 2½″	2, 3	A
	4	3¾″ × 3¾″ ◻	6	A, B
	4	4¾″ × 4¾″ ◻	8	A, B

S01-A

8

7

6

5

8

4

2

3

1

5

1

4

3

6

2

7

S01-B

Block-front drawings

Make 4.

A

B

Utah Star

～ STAR BLOCK 45 ～
Vermont Star

64 PIECES

The following fabric cutting list is for one star block.

Fabric	Number of Pieces	Piece Dimensions	Piece Number	Block Section
White/green print	8	2″ × 4″	1	A, B
Medium blue print	4	2″ × 4″	2	B
	4	1½″ × 4″	3	A
Dark blue	4	1½″ × 4″	3	B
	4	2″ × 4″	2	A
Medium green print	4	2″ × 6″	4	B
	4	2″ × 6″	4	A
Green/blue print	8	1¼″ × 4¾″	5	A, B
	4	1¼″ × 6½″	8*	A, B
White	4	3¼″ × 3¼″ ◻	6	A, B
	4	3¾″ × 3¾″ ◻	7	A, B
	2	4″ × 4″ ◻	9*	A, B

Add these pieces after sections A and B are joined. See page 18.

S45-A

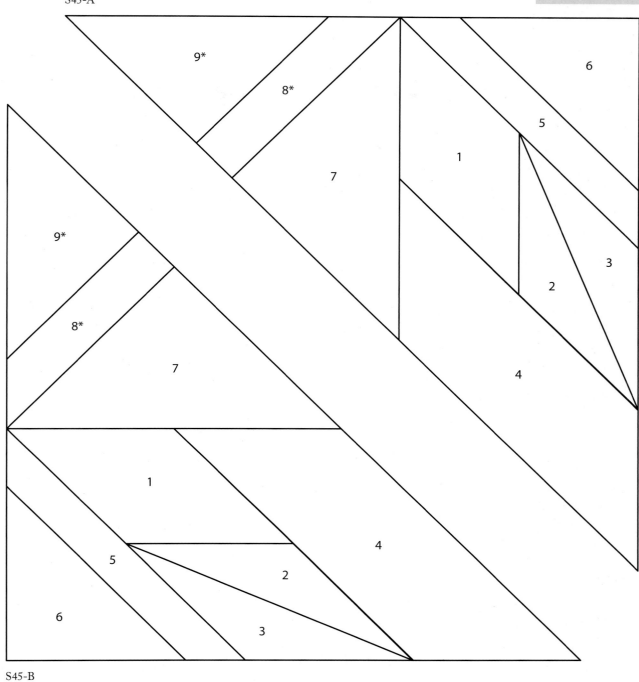

9*

8*

6

5

1

7

9*

3

2

8*

4

7

1

4

5

2

3

6

S45-B

Block-front drawings

Make 4.

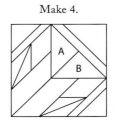

A

B

Vermont Star

~ STAR BLOCK 46 ~
# Virginia Star

56 PIECES

The following fabric cutting list is for one star block.

Fabric	Number of Pieces	Piece Dimensions	Piece Number	Block Section
Dark green	4	2″ × 4″	1	B
Black/red dot	4	2″ × 6″	3	B
Red	4	2″ × 3¾″	1	A
Rose print	4	2″ × 6″	3	A
Red/white stripe	8	2½″ × 2½″	4	A, B
	8	2″ × 2½″	2	A, B
	8	1¼″ × 4″	5, 6	A
White print	4	3¾″ × 3¾″ ◹	7	A
			5	B
	4	4¾″ × 4¾″ ◹	8	A
			6	B

S46-A

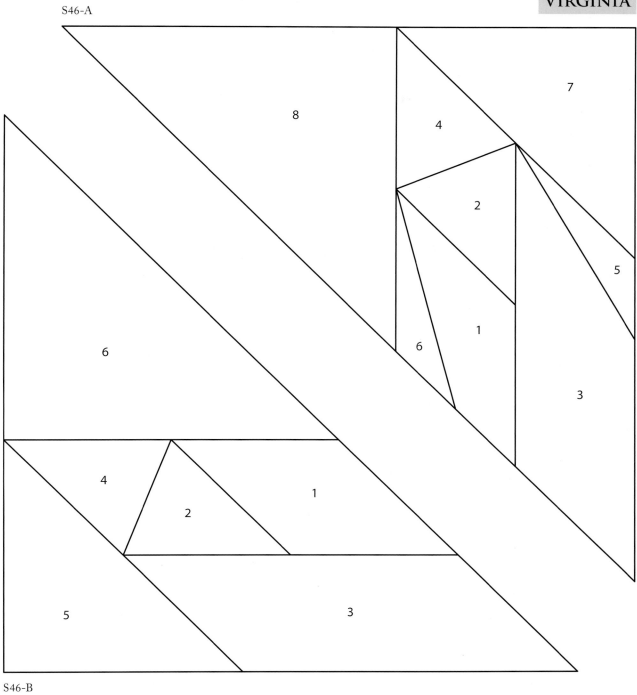

8

7

4

2

5

1

6

3

6

4

1

2

5

3

S46-B

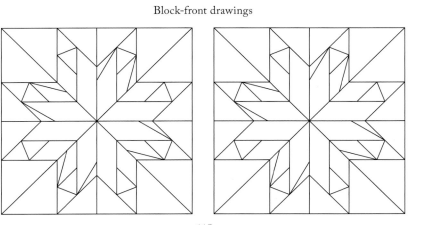

Block-front drawings

Make 4.

A

B

Virginia Star

STAR BLOCK 47

Washington Star

64 PIECES

The following fabric cutting list is for one star block.				
Fabric	Number of Pieces	Piece Dimensions	Piece Number	Block Section
Teal	8	2″ × 4″	2	A, B
Dark blue	8	2″ × 4½″	3	A, B
Yellow	8	2″ × 4″	1	A, B
	16	1½″ × 4″	4, 5	A, B
	8	2½″ × 2½″	6	A, B
Light blue print	4	3¾″ × 3¾″ ◹	7	A, B
	4	4¾″ × 4¾″ ◹	8	A, B

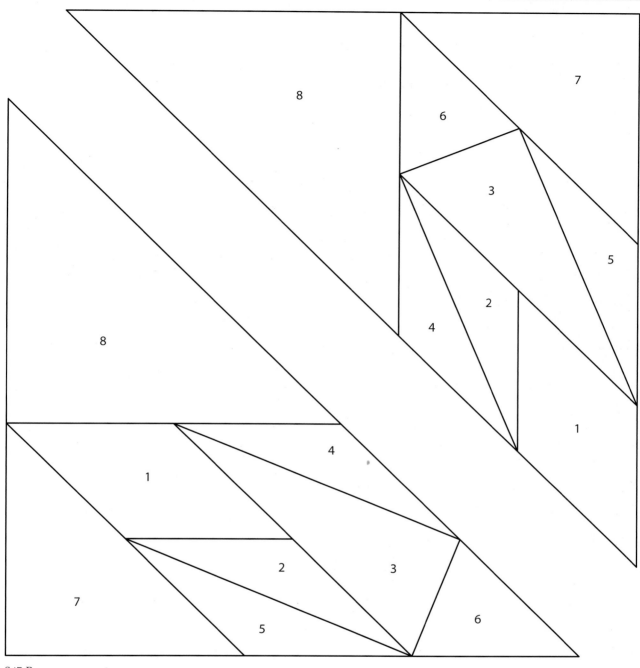

S47-A

8

7

6

3

5

2

4

8

1

1

4

2

3

7

5

6

S47-B

Block-front drawings

Make 4.

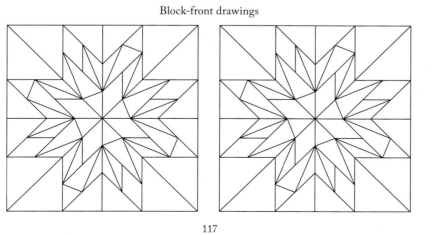

A

B

117

Washington Star

~ STAR BLOCK 48 ~
West Virginia Star

108 PIECES

> *The following fabric cutting list is for one star block.*

Fabric	Number of Pieces	Piece Dimensions	Piece Number	Block Section
Blue/pink print	8	2¼″ × 3″	1	A, B
Black/white print	8	1¼″ × 3″	11	A, B
Pink	16	1½″ × 3″	4, 5	A, B
Blue	16	1½″ × 3″	8, 9	A, B
	32	1½″ × 2″	2, 3, 6, 7	A, B
White	2	3″ × 3″ ◻	14*	A, B
	4	2½″ × 2½″ ◻	10	A, B
Black	4	3¾″ × 3¾″ ◻	12	A, B
	4	4¾″ × 4¾″ ◻	13	A, B

*Add these pieces after sections A and B are joined. See page 18.

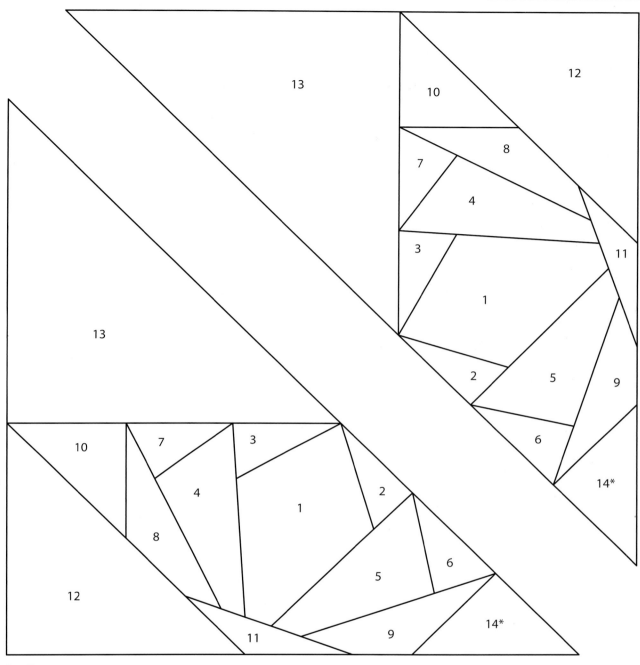

S48-A

13

12

10

8

7

4

3

11

1

2

5

9

6

14*

S48-B

13

10

7

3

4

1

2

8

6

5

12

11

9

14*

Block-front drawings

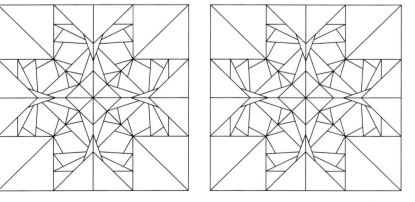

Make 4.

A

B

West Virginia Star

～ STAR BLOCK 49 ～
Wisconsin Star

56 PIECES

The following fabric cutting list is for one star block.

Fabric	Number of Pieces	Piece Dimensions	Piece Number	Block Section
White/green print	8	2½″ × 3½″	1	A, B
Blue square print	8	3″ × 3″	2	A, B
Yellow	8	1½″ × 2½″	3	A, B
Dark blue	8	1½″ × 3½″	4	A, B
Blue stripe	8	2½″ × 2½″	5	A, B
Blue/green print	4	3¾″ × 3¾″ ◪	6	A, B
	4	4¾″ × 4¾″ ◪	7	A, B

S49-A

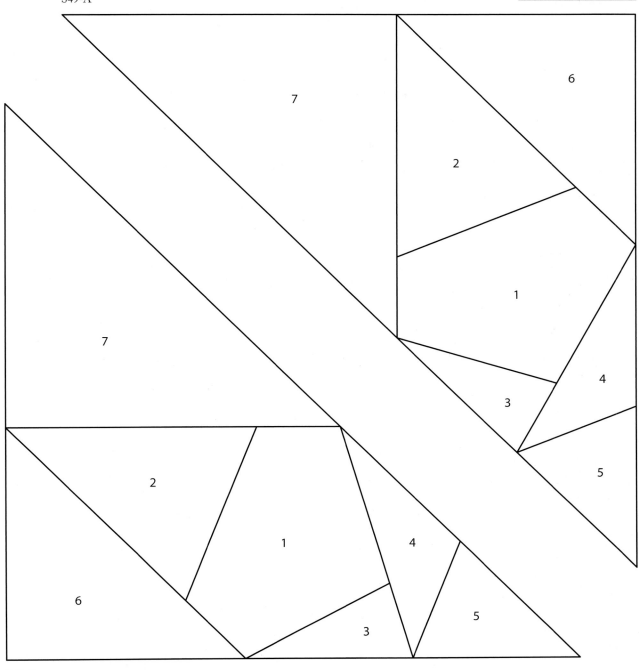

7

6

2

1

4

3

5

7

2

1

4

6

3

5

S49-B

Block-front drawings

Make 4.

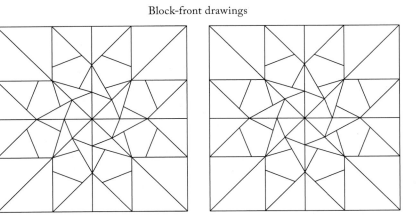

A

B

Wisconsin Star

~ STAR BLOCK 50 ~

Wyoming Star

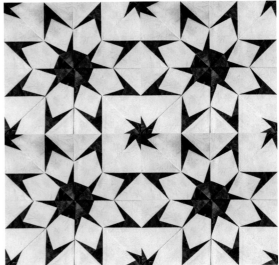

72 PIECES

The following fabric cutting list is for one star block.

Fabric	Number of Pieces	Piece Dimensions	Piece Number	Block Section
Medium Purple	4	1½″ × 3″	10	B
	8	1¼″ × 3″	2, 3	B
	8	2½″ × 2½″	4	A
			7	B
Dark Purple	8	2½″ × 2½″	5	A
			4	B
	4	1½″ × 3″	8	A
	16	1¼″ × 3″	2, 3	A
			5, 6	B
White	4	3¾″ × 3¾″	1	B
	4	3½″ × 4″	1	A
	4	3¾″ × 3¾″ ◻	6	A
			8	B
	4	4¾″ × 4¾″ ◻	7	A
			9	B

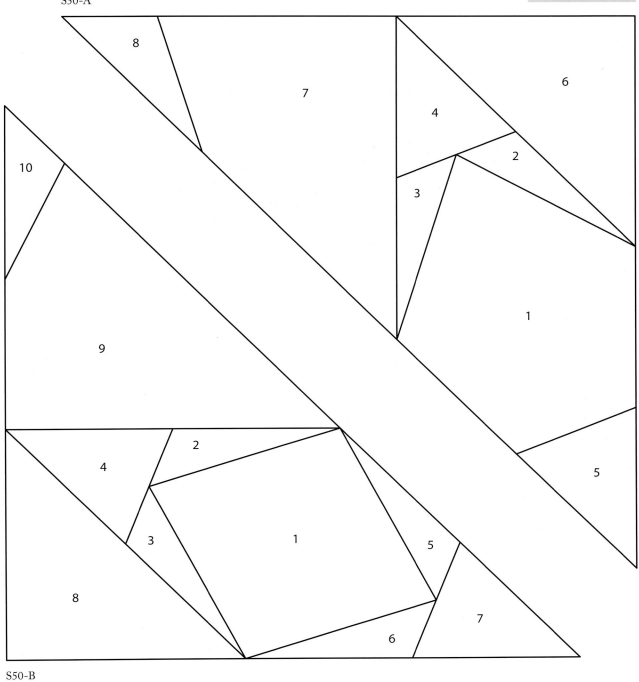

S50-A

8

7

6

4

2

3

10

9

1

2

4

3

1

5

5

8

3

7

6

S50-B

Block-front drawings

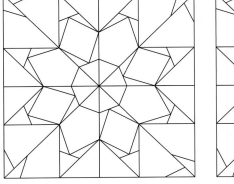

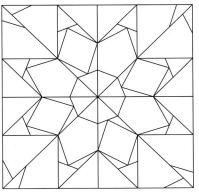

Make 4.

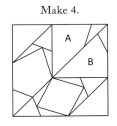

A

B

Wyoming Star

50 STATE STAR BLOCKS

~ STAR BLOCK 51 ~

Acadia National Park Star

64 PIECES

The following fabric cutting list is for one star block.

Fabric	Number of Pieces	Piece Dimensions	Piece Number	Block Section
Green	8	1½″ × 2½″	6	A, B
Rose	8	1½″ × 7″	4	A, B
Teal	4	2″ × 4¼″	1	B
	4	1½″ × 4½″	5	A
Light blue	4	2″ × 4¼″	1	A
	4	1½″ × 4½″	5	B
Black	8	2″ × 4″	3	A, B
	8	1½″ × 3″	2	A, B
	4	3¾″ × 3¾″ ◨	7	A, B
	4	4¾″ × 4¾″ ◨	8	A, B

S51-A

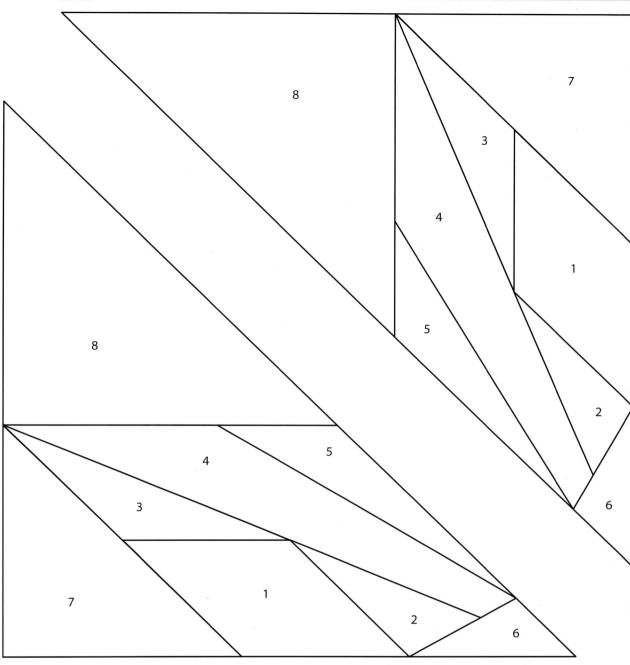

8

7

3

4

1

5

2

6

8

4

5

3

1

7

2

6

S51-B

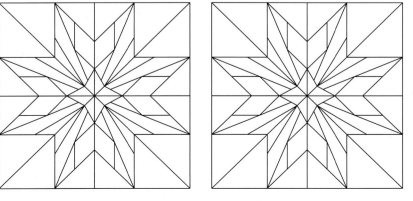

Block-front drawings

Make 4.

A

B

Acadia National Park Star

BONUS: 10 NATIONAL PARK STAR BLOCKS

Denali National Park Star

72 PIECES

The following fabric cutting list is for one star block.

Fabric	Number of Pieces	Piece Dimensions	Piece Number	Block Section
Light salmon	4	1½″ × 2½″	1	A
Medium salmon	4	1½″ × 2½″	1	B
White	8	1½″ × 3½″	3	A, B
	8	1½″ × 2½″	2	A, B
	16	1½″ × 4¼″	6, 7	A, B
Dark blue	8	1¾″ × 5½″	5	A, B
Medium blue	8	2″ × 4″	4	A, B
Yellow	4	3¾″ × 3¾″ ◻	8	A, B
	4	4¾″ × 4¾″ ◻	9	A, B

S52-A

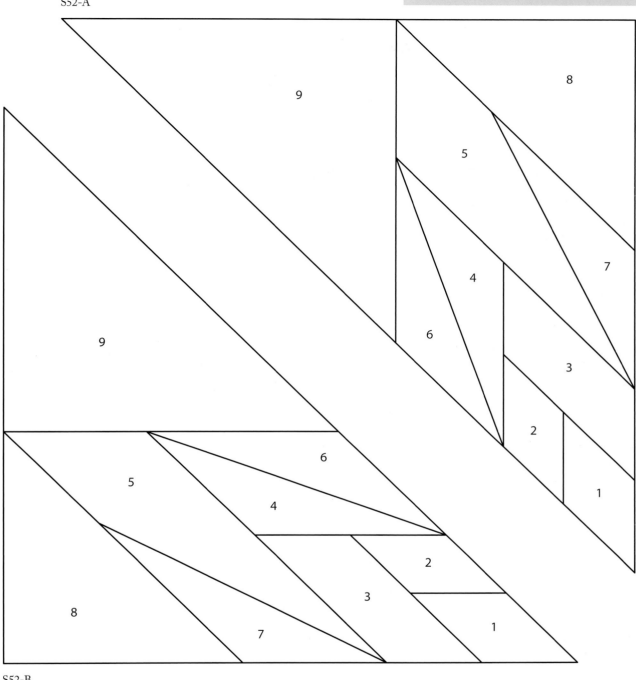

S52-B

Block-front drawings

Make 4.

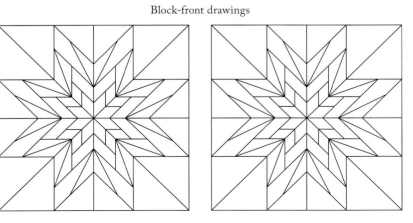

Denali National Park Star

Everglades National Park Star

88 PIECES

The following fabric cutting list is for one star block.

Fabric	Number of Pieces	Piece Dimensions	Piece Number	Block Section
Yellow	8	2¾″ × 2¾″	1	A, B
	16	1¼″ × 3¼″	6, 7	A, B
Medium rose	8	2½″ × 2½″	8	A, B
Purple print	8	1½″ × 2¾″	2	A, B
Purple	8	1½″ × 3½″	3	A, B
Medium green	8	1¼″ × 4″	4	A, B
Dark green	8	1¼″ × 5″	5	A, B
Dark rose	8	1¾″ × 4½″	11	A, B
Green print	4	3¾″ × 3¾″ ◹	9	A, B
	4	4¾″ × 4¾″ ◹	10	A, B

S53-A

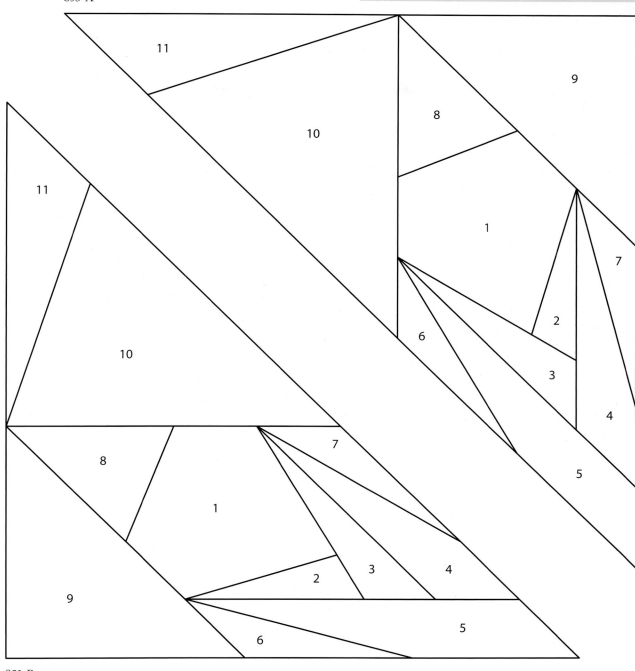

S53-B

Block-front drawings

Make 4.

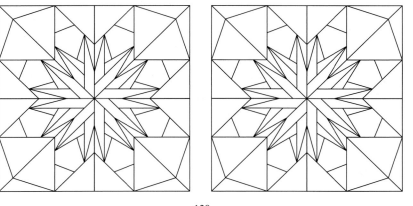

Everglades National Park Star

~ STAR BLOCK 54 ~
# Glacier National Park Star

~ **100 PIECES** ~

The following fabric cutting list is for one star block.

Fabric	Number of Pieces	Piece Dimensions	Piece Number	Block Section
	8	2¼″ × 2¼″	4	A, B
White	16	2″ × 2¾″	2, 3	A, B
	32	1¼″ × 3″	6, 7, 9, 10	A, B
Blue #1	8	2″ × 2½″	1	A, B
Blue #2	8	2″ × 3¾″	5	A, B
	2	2½″ × 2½″ ◹	13*	A, B
Blue #3	8	1¾″ × 2¾″	8	A, B
Blue #4	4	3¾″ × 3¾ ◹	11	A, B
	4	4¾″ × 4¾″ ◹	12	A, B

*Add these pieces after sections A and B are joined. See page 18.

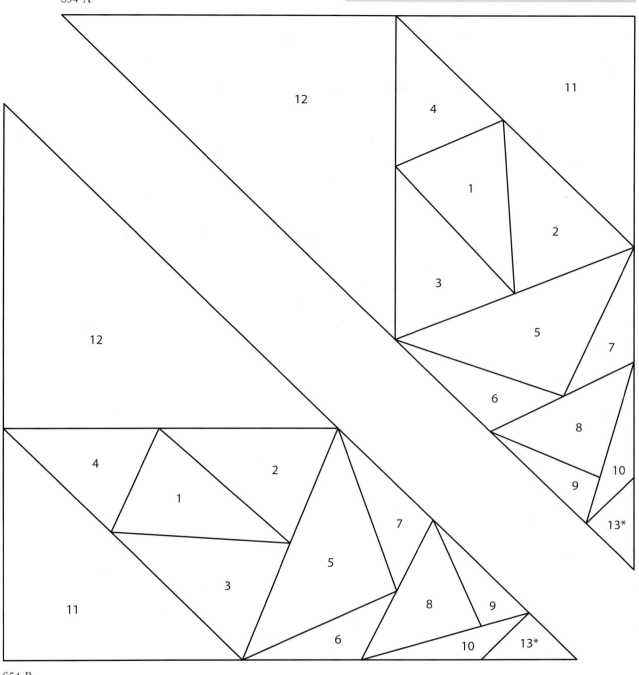

S54-A

S54-B

Block-front drawings

Make 4.

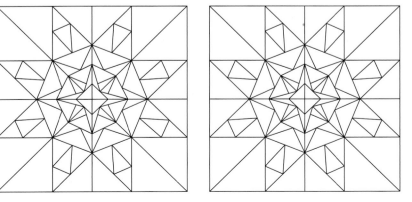

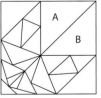

BONUS: 10 NATIONAL PARK STAR BLOCKS

~ STAR BLOCK 55 ~

Grand Canyon National Park Star

72 PIECES

The following fabric cutting list is for one star block.

Fabric	Number of Pieces	Piece Dimensions	Piece Number	Block Section
Peach	8	1½″ × 3½″	3	A, B
	8	1½″ × 2¼″	2	A, B
Turquoise	8	1½″ × 2¼″	1	A, B
Brown	16	2″ × 3″	4, 5	A, B
Beige	8	2¼″ × 3¾″	6	A, B
Rust	8	2½″ × 2½″	7	A, B
Multi-color print	4	3¾″ × 3¾″ ◻	8	A, B
	4	4¾″ × 4¾″ ◻	9	A, B

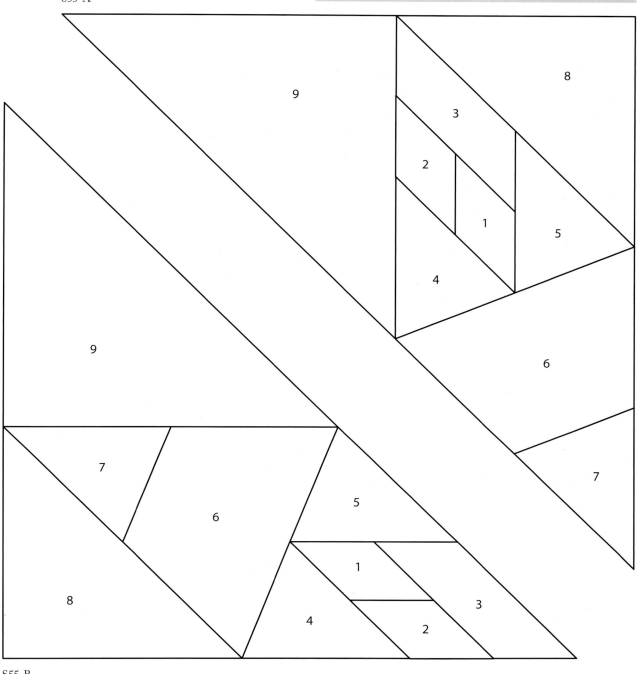

S55-A

9

8

3

2

1

5

4

9

6

7

6

7

5

8

1

4

2

3

S55-B

Block-front drawings

Make 4.

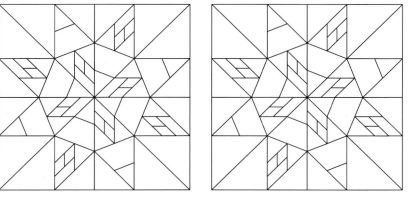

A

B

Grand Canyon National Park Star

BONUS: 10 NATIONAL PARK STAR BLOCKS

Mount Rainier National Park Star

88 PIECES

The following fabric cutting list is for one star block.

Fabric	Number of Pieces	Piece Dimensions	Piece Number	Block Section
Rose	8	2¼″ × 2¼″	6	A, B
Yellow	8	1½″ × 2½″	1	A, B
Black	16	2″ × 2¾″	4, 5	A, B
Stripe	8	2¼″ × 4″	7	A, B
Medium blue	8	1¾″ × 4½″	9	A, B
Light blue	8	1½″ × 3½″	8	A, B
	16	1¼″ × 1¾″	2, 3	A, B
White	4	3¾″ × 3¾″ ◩	10	A, B
	4	4¾″ × 4¾″ ◩	11	A, B

S56-A

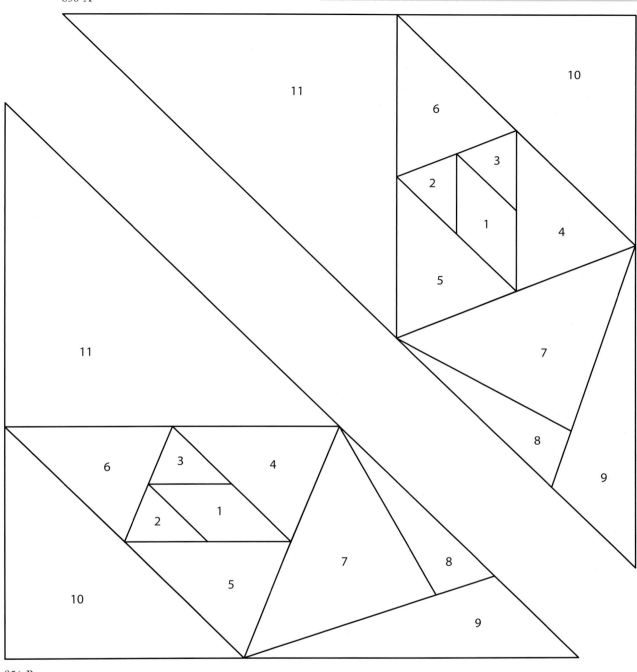

S56-B

Block-front drawings

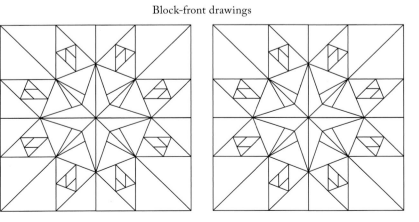

Make 4.

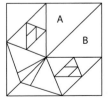

Mount Rainier National Park Star

BONUS: 10 NATIONAL PARK STAR BLOCKS

Redwood National Park Star

72 PIECES

The following fabric cutting list is for one star block.

Fabric	Number of Pieces	Piece Dimensions	Piece Number	Block Section
Assorted colors	8	2½″ × 2½″	7	A, B
	8	2″ × 4″	2	A, B
	8	1¼″ × 4½″	3	A, B
	8	1¼″ × 3″	4	A, B
White print	8	2″ × 4″	1	A, B
	16	1½″ × 4″	5, 6	A, B
Dark red	4	3¾″ × 3¾″ ◻	8	A, B
	4	4¾″ × 4¾″ ◻	9	A, B

S57-A

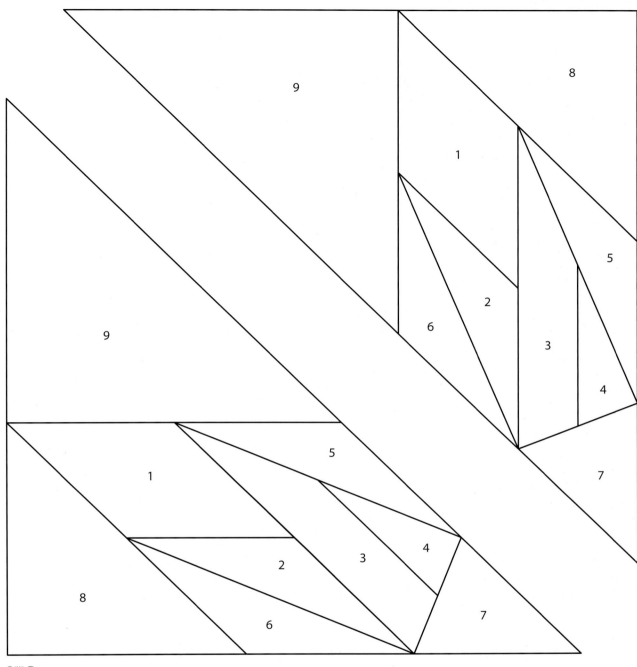

S57-B

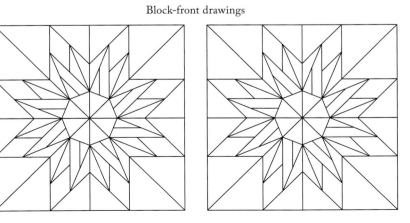

Block-front drawings

Make 4.

Redwood National Park Star

Rocky Mountain National Park Star

128 PIECES

The following fabric cutting list is for one star block.

Fabric	Number of Pieces	Piece Dimensions	Piece Number	Block Section
Dark purple	8	1½″ × 2½″	1	A, B
	32	1″ × 2½″	4, 5, 8, 9	A, B
White stripe	8	1¼″ × 3½″	3	A, B
	8	1¼″ × 2¼″	2	A, B
Medium green	16	1¼″ × 2½″	6, 7	A, B
	4	1½″ × 4″	12	B
Light green	16	1¼″ × 2″	10, 11	A, B
	4	1½″ × 4″	12	A
Medium purple	8	1½″ × 3½″	14	A, B
	4	3¾″ × 3¾″ ◻	15	A, B
Light green print	4	4¾″ × 4¾″ ◻	16	A, B
	8	2¼″ × 3½″	13	A, B

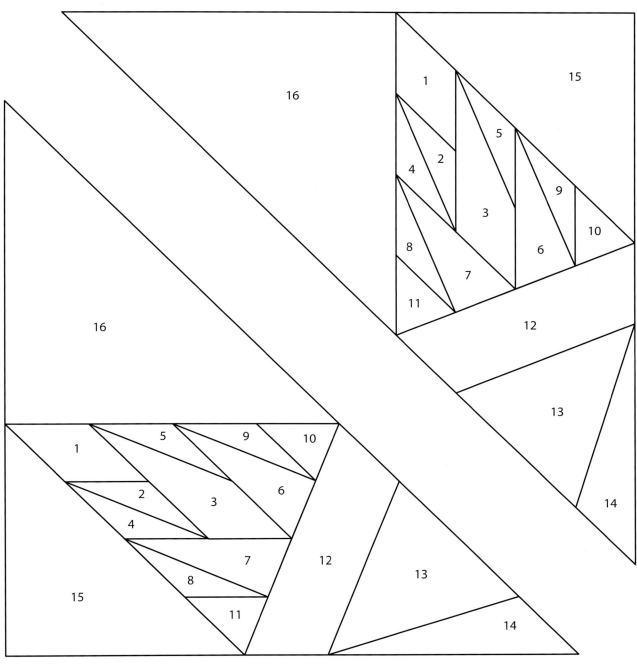

S58-A

S58-B

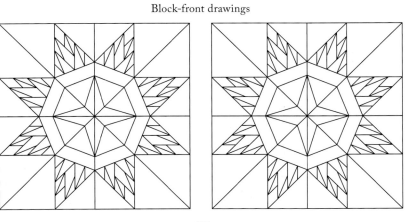

Block-front drawings

Make 4.

A

B

Rocky Mountain National Park Star

BONUS: 10 NATIONAL PARK STAR BLOCKS

STAR BLOCK 59

Yellowstone National Park Star

72 PIECES

The following fabric cutting list is for one star block.

Fabric	Number of Pieces	Piece Dimensions	Piece Number	Block Section
Beige	8	2″ × 4″	1	A, B
	16	1½″ × 3½″	4, 5	A, B
Dark brown	8	1¼″ × 4″	3	A, B
Medium brown	8	1½″ × 3½″	2	A, B
Blue	8	1½″ × 3″	6	A, B
Blue print	8	2½″ × 4½″	7	A, B
Beige print	4	3¾″ × 3¾″ ⧅	8	A, B
	4	4¾″ × 4¾″ ⧅	9	A, B

S59-A

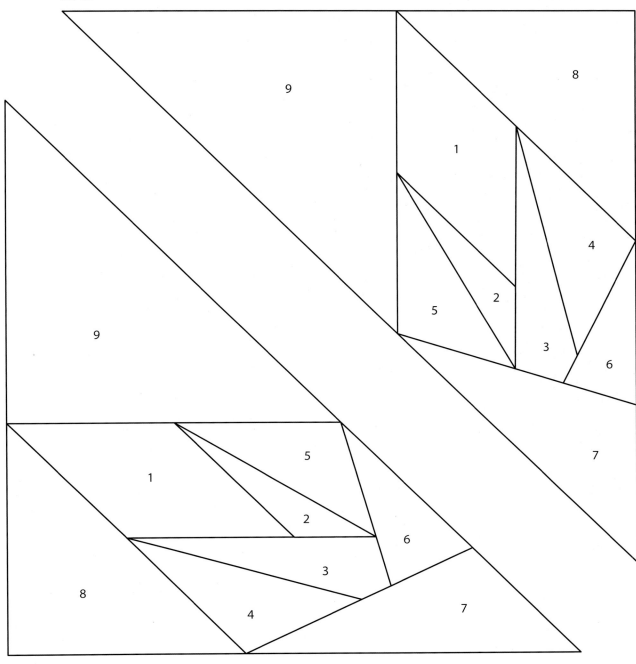

S59-B

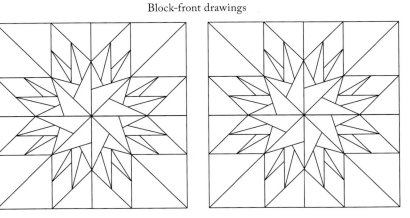

Block-front drawings

Make 4.

Yellowstone National Park Star

BONUS: 10 NATIONAL PARK STAR BLOCKS

~ STAR BLOCK 60 ~
# Zion National Park Star

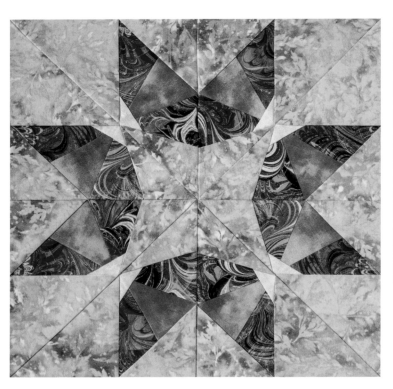

56 PIECES

The following fabric cutting list is for one star block.

Fabric	Number of Pieces	Piece Dimensions	Piece Number	Block Section
Gold	8	1¼″ × 3″	4	A, B
Orange	8	2½″ × 3″	2	A, B
Orange print	8	2¼″ × 3½″	3	A, B
	8	2¼″ × 3¾″	1	A, B
	4	3¾″ × 3¾″ �****️	6	A, B
Green	4	4¾″ × 4¾″ ◻️	7	A, B
	8	2½″ × 4½″	5	A, B

S60-A

7

6

1

2

4

3

5

7

1

4

2

6

3

5

S60-B

Block-front drawings

Make 4.

A

B

Zion National Park Star

BONUS: 10 NATIONAL PARK STAR BLOCKS

ABOUT THE AUTHOR

Carol Doak discovered her love of quilting in 1979 when she took a seven-week basic quilting class in Worthington, Ohio. She taught that class the following year and discovered that she also loved to teach others how to make quilts. Since then she has taught more than a million people to quilt through her best-selling books and DVDs and by traveling to teach around the world.

An innovator in the industry, Carol continues to wow the quilting world with her creative uses for paper piecing. Since writing her first paper piecing book in 1993, she has designed more than 1,000 paper-pieced designs.

Her passion for designing and teaching is evident, whether you have taken a class from her or learned from her books and DVDs.

Visit Carol online!

Website: caroldoak.com

Other titles from Carol Doak:

Carol Doak's Foundation Paper is available from:

C&T Publishing, Inc., ctpub.com or ask for them at your local quilt shop

Other paper piecing books authored by Carol and available from C&T Publishing:

Show Me How to Paper Piece

Carol Doak's Creative Combinations

50 Little Paper-Pieced Blocks

Mariner's Compass Stars

40 Bright & Bold Paper-Pieced Blocks

Carol Doak's Simply Sensational 9-Patch Stars